DATE DUE

MR 20 '97			

DEMCO 38-296

Teachers and Librarians
Working Together

Teachers and Librarians Working Together: To Make Students Lifelong Library Users

by

Linda R. Sparks

and

Barbara Sorrow

WITH A FOREWORD BY
THE HON. NED MCWHERTER,
GOVERNOR OF TENNESSEE

McFarland & Company, Inc., Publishers
Jefferson, North Carolina, and London

British Library Cataloguing-in-Publication data are available

Library of Congress Cataloguing-in-Publication Data

Sparks, Linda R.
    Teachers and librarians working together : to make students
lifelong library users / by Linda R. Sparks and Barbara Sorrow.
        p.   cm.
    Includes bibliographical references and index.
    ISBN 0-89950-649-6 (sewn softcover : 55# alk. paper) ∞
    1. High school students — Library orientation.   2. High school
libraries — Activity programs.   3. Youth — Books and reading.
I. Sorrow, Barbara.   II. Title.
Z675.S3S732   1991
025.5'678223 — dc20   91-52837
                                                       CIP

Manufactured in the United States of America

McFarland & Company, Inc., Publishers
  Box 611, Jefferson, North Carolina 28640

*Dedicated
to
the students of Tennessee*

Foreword

The Hon. Ned McWherter
Governor of Tennessee

When I was growing up in the small, rural West Tennessee town of Palmersville, life was simple — movies were a quarter, sodas were a nickel, walking to the country store was a way of life, and getting an education was easy.

My friends and I knew that we could get an education, settle down in Palmersville, find a good job and support a family. We knew that the basic skills we learned in school would see us through the coming years. We knew that we would be prepared to go on to college or to learn a trade.

But with each passing day, our technology has become more advanced and our economy has become a global one. No longer are our children and grandchildren able to support themselves with a bare-minimum education.

The backyard-mechanic, who used to learn his skills through trial and error or through the teaching of a local mechanic, no longer exists. With today's modern technology, complicated electrical systems and computer systems have replaced manual door locks, windows, stereo systems and thermostats. Repairing a car takes much more than a "trial-and-error" education. At the end of my first term as governor, I traveled throughout the state and visited schools in every school district in Tennessee. I saw bright, talented students and hard working teachers doing the best they could with the resources they had. But as I talked with teachers, students, principals and parents, I saw great concern in their eyes and heard dwindling hope in their voices for the generation of tomorrow. No longer can we afford to train our young people for a 21st century economy in schools designed for a time and place that no longer exists.

That is why I dedicated my second term as governor of this great state to the children of Tennessee. I am wholly dedicated to restoring the hope of our children — the hope of being prepared to find a job, of being able to compete in a global economy and of being able to enjoy the blessings that economic growth has brought to Tennessee.

The issue is far broader than a simple desire to secure more funds for education. It involves fundamental changes in how we teach and what we expect our students to learn. It means restructuring our schools to adapt to the skills needed in an economy of increasing technology.

Our hope for the future of this state and nation rests in our hands. With the stakes so high, we cannot afford to lose the fight.

Table of Contents

We dream of a society
that will benefit all people.
We dream of schools
that will benefit all students.
We dream of students
who will benefit society.

I. Library Literacy

A variety of flexible activities will be introduced in this chapter. Each teacher can use these ideas to reinforce basic library skills. These activities are user-oriented and more enjoyable than teacher or librarian lectures.

The activities in this chapter flow from one to another. Through role playing, the student can experience the library process and understand the importance of the teacher, librarian, and student working together. When the teacher makes her expectations concerning library behavior clear in a humorous way, many problems that might otherwise occur are thwarted. The student goes to the library for the first time and, in this orientation process, browses and becomes acquainted with the layout, rules, and major areas of the library. For several days following this initial visit, the students will work with groups in data stations utilizing a variety of tactual and challenging activities. The culmination of the process involves reviewing library terminology through playing charades.

Each teacher should extract the aspects of this section which he finds most valuable and useful in his particular teaching situation.

Role Playing

An activity to introduce before actually going to the library is role playing, which can be used in both the personal and social aspects of education. The purpose of role playing is to help the student find personal meaning inside the social system and within his own problems. It helps students analyze social problems, and make good judgments concerning them. Teachers and students are constantly faced with interpersonal and social dilemmas.

Role playing is facing problems through action: a problem is exposed, acted out, and talked about. Some or all of the students can participate. Those not actually participating, the observers, can still experience emotional response from the role playing. Since this book deals directly with the library experience, we hope to provide an activity that will be beneficial to the librarian as well as to the student.

1

To begin the role playing exercise, the teacher must decide if the entire class or only a few participants will enact the scene. Involving the entire class often may create a busy interaction, but the benefits are great because everyone gets to experience the release of feelings by actually taking part.

To begin, the teacher should ask the students to number one, two, one, two, etc., all the way around the room. The teacher should ask all of the number ones to raise their hands. Each number one should have a number two partner. This can be accomplished in several ways. Tell all of the number ones to choose a number two, or tell the number ones that they are partners with the number two directly behind or closest to them. Ensure that no one is left out. If there is an extra person, let her be partners with a group. Students can stand or sit to do this activity. If students stand, the ones can get in a circle (facing out) and the twos can get in a circle around the ones. The partners should be facing each other.

The teacher should then say: "Number ones, raise your hand. You are a high school student who has trouble staying on task. You have several assignments that you should be working on, but you would rather be reading or talking with your friends. You *do* plan on finishing your library assignment *someday,* but it is due at the end of the period."

"Number twos, raise your hand. You are the librarian and have been walking around the library from table to table, asking students if they need assistance. You want to tell this young person to get busy and use his time wisely. You know the assignment is due at the end of the period. You don't want to be too pushy or overbearing. You want this teenager to have a positive library experience."

After one minute, call time. Sometimes it is hard to regain control. Tell everyone that it is time to change roles.

Role play number two: "Number twos, raise your hand. You are now a teacher who wants to send twelve to fifteen students to the library all afternoon to read magazines. You are going to be busy working on the prom activities in your classroom, and all of the students have promised to behave."

"Number ones, raise your hand. You are the librarian. You have a full library of students (over 100), all working on different things. The copy machine keeps jamming. You are trying to check on the VCRs and TVs that seem to be missing. The Alumni Committee is working in the back corner, twelve kids are lined up waiting to check out books, and the superintendent is visiting the school today. You are stressed to the breaking point. The twelve to fifteen students do not have an assignment and do not need to be in the library on this day. Hold your ground; be firm."

"Number twos, be pushy, call in any favors, use politics. Does everyone understand? You have one minute to make your arguments. Begin."

Time should be called after one minute. Have students return to their seats.

The purpose of this activity is to help students understand the dilemma that the librarian is often in, and to help make them aware of behaviors that they can exemplify to make the library experience a positive one. Most teenagers have no idea about the intricacies involved in running and monitoring a library. Perhaps through role playing, the students can understand how important it is for *everyone* to cooperate, be dependable, and work independently.

Even though role playing may seem like a junior high or even elementary activity, it is not. Secondary students also should be given guidelines to go by in the library. They need to be shown specific examples of leadership. Role playing is a non-threatening way to give examples of expectations. Role playing is often a very effective way to get positive results.

Teachers' Expectations

The teacher should be responsible for establishing and clarifying rules to follow at all times.

At the beginning of the year, before going to the library the first time, the teacher should explain and clarify library rules. This can be done in any number of ways. The usual way is that the teacher says, "Don't talk. Don't push. Don't disturb anyone." But a more creative and humorous approach to insuring good behavior can be used.

When students know what to expect, and when somewhat humorous examples are used to make them see themselves, the results are usually very positive. There is no need to threaten students. Escort them to the library, and especially the first few visits, help set a precedent of work, calmness, and maturity. Brag on those who are on task instead of scolding the person off task. Try to be positive. That is a big part of being a successful teacher and librarian. Our goal is for the student to become a lifetime library user. Having positive library experiences is a step in that direction.

How to Coalesce
by
Ann & Andy

Teachers' Expectations

I. It is a privilege to get to go to the library.
   A. Going to the library is not mandated by the county or state curriculum.
   B. The principal has made no statement about school policy requiring students to spend time in the library.
   C. It is easier for me to stay in the classroom and lecture: there is less space to cover and a more controlled environment.
   D. I sacrifice my instructional time to allow you to go to the library because I know you will need to know independent research skills later in your education, and I care about you and your future.
II. As you know, people display certain behavior in certain situations.
   A. For instance, when the preacher comes to visit you at home, you act more refined.
      1. You dress up.
      2. You use proper manners.
      3. You don't stretch out in front of the television and crank up MTV.
   B. When you are at a pep rally, you may act bizarre.
      1. You scream and holler.
      2. You jump up and down and do the wave.
      3. You throw confetti.
      4. You act crazy; it is okay.
   C. When you go to the movies with your sweetie, a certain behavior is permissible.
      1. It is all right to look cross-eyed at each other.
      2. Holding hands is the norm.
   D. But, in the *library*, there is another code of ethics.
      1. There is no loud talking; be considerate of those studying and work quietly.
      2. Sit two to a table when possible, and do not sit with your chit-chatting friends.
      3. Get the book or materials that you need, then sit down and work with them without having to be constantly monitored by the librarian or teacher.
      4. No coagulation behind the reference stacks; move on and take care of your own business.
      5. Ask for help only after you have exhausted all possible means that you know about.
      6. Clean up the area around your table before you leave—every piece of paper—and push your chair up under the table neatly.
      7. The same rules apply in the library as in the classroom.
         A. Be courteous.
         B. Do your best work.
      8. Walk to and from the library like young ladies and gentlemen, not like parched buffaloes making a run for the watering hole.
      9. Try to conduct yourself in a mature manner.

Orientation

Orientation is an instructional introduction that will help the student become acquainted with the library. Instruction should begin with planning which involves both the librarian and teacher. The students' orientation should be positive and informative. Students have told us that librarians should not concentrate on the card catalog and classification systems. So, try a different approach, one that involves humor, challenging skills, flexibility, and interdisciplinary activities. However, do not just discard Dewey.

Initially, the students will come to the library from each class (history, sociology, science, English, etc.) to become familiar with the materials and resources which will support that specific discipline. The student will concentrate on the classification area and subject headings which promote that discipline. Each student will receive a handbook and a map of the library at this time. Included in the handbook will be information about the Dewey Decimal and/or Library of Congress classification systems. A video presentation should be available for the students if they want additional information or for the physically handicapped students who may not be able to browse. Closed-circuit television can be installed so the students can see themselves as they search for resources. Students enjoy seeing themselves.

During this first visit to the library the librarian and teacher will instruct briefly about the layout of the library and specific resources available therein. Each student will receive an assignment on her particular subject area. The librarian and the teacher will be available to help the students with their initial search. By actually searching in a hands-on manner, the student will remember where the resources are located, and will be able to transfer this knowledge to any specific discipline: history, science, English, sociology, religion.

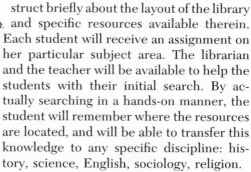

The teacher and librarian should make the initial search both informative and enjoyable. Topics such as *1960s Personalities* or current events, which are of particular interest to a specific group, may make the search more enjoyable for the student. The number and the questions can be determined by the academic level of the students. For example, an easy search question might be: What if Ernest Hemingway wanted a

Dewey Decimal System

The call number or book's address is located on the spine of each book or on the front of other media, such as computer disks, audio/visual materials, etc.

000 Generalities
010 Bibliographies & catalogs
020 Library science
030 General encyclopedic works
040 General essays
050 General periodicals
060 General organizations
070 Newspapers & journalism
080 General collections
090 Manuscripts & book rarities

100 Philosophy & related
110 Ontology & methodology
120 Knowledge, cause, purpose, man
130 Pseudo- & parapsychology
140 Specific philosophic viewpoints
150 Psychology
160 Logic
170 Ethics (Moral philosophy)
180 Ancient, med., Oriental philos.
190 Modern Western philosophy

200 Religion
210 Natural religion
220 Bible
230 Christian doctrinal theology
240 Christ. moral & dev. theology
250 Christ. pastoral, paroch., etc.
260 Christ. social & eccles. theol.
270 Hist. & geog. of Christ. church
280 Christ. denominations & sects
290 Other religions & compar. rel.

300 The Social sciences
310 Statistical method & statistics
320 Political science
330 Economics
340 Law
350 Public administration
360 Welfare & association
370 Education
380 Commerce
390 Customs & folklore

400 Language
410 Linguistics & nonverbal lang.
420 English & Anglo-Saxon
430 Germanic languages
440 French, Provencal, Catalan
450 Italian, Romanian, etc.
460 Spanish & Portuguese
470 Italic languages
480 Classical & Greek
490 Other languages

500 Pure sciences
510 Mathematics
520 Astronomy & allied sciences
530 Physics
540 Chemistry & allied sciences
550 Earth sciences
560 Paleontology
570 Anthropolog. & biol. sciences
580 Botanical sciences
590 Zoological sciences

600 Technology (applied sciences)
610 Medical sciences
620 Engineering & allied operations
630 Agriculture & agric. industries
640 Domestic arts & sciences
650 Business & related enterprises
660 Chemical technology, etc.
670 Manufactures processible
680 Assembled & final products
690 Buildings

700 The arts
710 Civic & landscape art
720 Architecture
730 Sculpture & plastic arts
740 Drawing & decorative arts
750 Painting & paintings
760 Graphic arts
770 Photography & photographs
780 Music
790 Recreation (recreational arts)

800 Literature & rhetoric
810 American lit. in English
820 Engl. & Anglo-Saxon literature
830 Germanic languages literature
840 French, Provencal, Catalan lit.
850 Italian, Romanian, etc.
860 Spanish & Portuguese lit.
870 Italic languages literature
880 Classical & Greek literature
890 Lits. of other languages

900 General geog. & history, etc.
910 General geography
920 General biog., geneal., etc.
930 Gen. hist. of ancient world
940 Gen. hist. of modern world
950 Gen. hist. of modern Asia
960 Gen. hist. of modern Africa
970 Gen. hist. of North America
980 Gen. hist. of South America
990 Gen. hist. of rest of world

Library of Congress
Classification System

The call number is located on the spine of each book or on the front of other media. The call number consists of the letter (or letters) representing the subject area or subtopic the media covers and a series of other letters and numbers that identify the specific media you are looking for.

A General works

B Philosophy & Religion
   BD Metaphysics
   BF Psychology
   BJ Ethics
   BM Judaism
   BR Christianity

C History (General—Civilization, Genealogy)

D History—Old World
   DA Great Britain
   DC France
   DE Classical antiquity
   DF Greece
   DK Russia
   DS Asia
   DT Africa

E American history & general U.S. history

F American history (local) & Latin American

G Geography, anthropology, folklore, sports & other

H Social sciences
   HA   Statistics
   HB–HJ Finance
   HM   Sociology
   HQ   Family, marriage, home
   HV   Social pathology

J Political science

K Law

L Education

M Music

N Fine Arts
   NA Architecture
   NB Sculpture
   ND Painting

P Language & literature
   PA Classical language & lit.
   PB Celtic language
   PC Romance language
   PD Germanic language
   PE English language
   PN Literary history & collections
   PQ Romance literature
   PR English literature
   PS American literature
   PT Teutonic literature
   PZ Fiction & Juvenile literature

Q Science
   QA Mathematics
   QB Astronomy
   QC Physics
   QD Chemistry
   QE Geology
   QH Natural History
   QK Botany
   QL Zoology
   QM Human anatomy
   QP Physiology
   QR Bacteriology

R Medicine
   RD Surgery
   RS Pharmacy
   RT Nursing

S Agriculture, forestry, animal culture, fish culture, hunting

T Technology

U Military Science

V Naval Science

Z Bibliography and Library Science

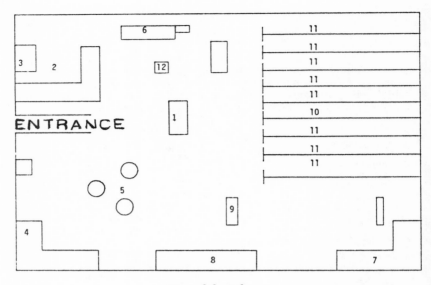

Map of the Library

1. Reference Librarian
2. Circulation Librarian
3. Books on Reserve
4. Card Catalog
5. Index Tables
6. Copier

7. Current Magazines
8. Newspapers
9. Atlas Case
10. Reference Books
11. Circulating Books
12. Pencil Sharpener

fictitious book about the sea? Locate one in the card catalog and provide the following bibliographic information: title, author, and publisher. A more advanced "What if" might be: What if Ernest Hemingway wanted information about the lifestyles of village people in Cuba during the 1950s? Find several sources which could help him, and write the following bibliographic information for each: title, author, copyright date, and place of publication. Does this source have a bibliography?

The students should be given a chance to look around the library. They may be looking for specific information and the following hand-out can help them.

The following two hand-outs, If? and Creative Writing, are activities that can be used to assist the student in becoming familiar with library resources.

Performance Based Tests

Students are often given pre- and post-tests to determine competency in library skills. These test results are sometimes misleading.

A   Are you searching for?

R

E   Background or
         Biographical ──────── ⌈Encyclopedia
         Information

Y

O

U

S

E   Facts   ⌈Dictionary

A   Definitions   Handbook

R   Brief information   ⌊Atlas

C

H

I

N   Books   ⌈Card catalog

G   Resources   ⌊Online catalog

F

O   Up-to-date   ⌈Periodical indexes

R   information ──────── ⌊CD ROM-Database

?

If?

The sixties were a unique time in American history. The people were fascinating and had their own individual styles which continue to make a statement today. Read the following statements and find as much information as you can in the time allowed. Use your map and handbook if necessary. Ask the teacher and librarian if you need help.

1. If John F. Kennedy needed a book on the U.S. Constitution, where would he go to begin his search? _____

2. If John Steinbeck wanted information about people during the Great Depression, what would be the most appropriate subject heading under which to look? ____

3. If James Dean needed information about repairing motorcycles, what would be a reliable source?_____
   Title: _____
   Author: _____ Call #: _____

4. If Jimi Hendrix wanted to know the location of Woodstock, where could he find this information? _____
   Which encyclopedia did you use to find background information on Woodstock?
   _____
   Which Atlas shows the location of Woodstock? _____

5. If Elvis Presley wanted a book on rock and roll, he could browse in the 700 classification area and locate a book he might enjoy. What would it be? _____
   Title: _____
   Author: _____

6. If Martin Luther King needed a book on civil rights, which classification (name and number) would he use? _____
   _____

7. If the Beatles needed information on the hippies for the peace movement, they could go to the *Readers' Guide to Periodical Literature* on the index table and find information.
   Name of Article: _____
   Author: _____ Name of Magazine: _____
   Date of Magazine: _____ Page #: _____
   Do we have this magazine? _____

8. If Lyndon B. Johnson needed a book on Vietnam, he could find a source in the history section. Name one._____
   Title/Author: _____

9. If you were living in the sixties, what five dynamic people could you find listed in the Current Biography? Tell why you are interested in them.
   (A) Name _____ (D) Name _____
   (B) Name_____(E) Name_____
   (C) Name _____

10. If Marilyn Monroe needed a book review on *The Crucible* or *Death of a Salesman*, she could go to the text on microfiche to see if she could find a review for either one. She could look under *The Crucible* or *Death of a Salesman* or Arthur Miller.
    Name of Magazine:_____
    Author: _____
    Date of Magazine: _____ Page #: _____
    Why would she look under Arthur Miller? _____

    ****EXTRA CREDIT (10 points)****
    Why do you think Marilyn Monroe would be interested in either of these dramas?
    Where could you look to find this information? _____

Creative Writing

Find information about a sixties personality and answer the following "If?" questions. Write a 300 word composition about one of them. Be creative!

1. If Elvis Presley were alive today, his job or profession might be: _____
   BECAUSE: _____
   _____
   _____
   _____
   _____

2. If Marilyn Monroe were alive today and owned a car, it would probably be a _____
   BECAUSE: _____
   _____
   _____
   _____
   _____

3. If the Beatles were all alive today, their favorite song might be: _____
   BECAUSE: _____
   _____
   _____
   _____
   _____

In secondary schools when these tests are given, a student may score extremely high according to his previous library experience. The librarian may feel satisfied that the student understands how to use the library.

When this same student gets to the college level, however, the English professor or college librarian may report that he cannot utilize library resources. He may have difficulty using indexes, narrowing broad subject headings, finding resources independently, and, in general, using the library.

Because of these obvious inadequacies, it might be advantageous for librarians to use performance based testing. This includes any type of hands-on activity where the student has to use the multitude of resources and media in the library. The activities in this chapter could be used as performance based tests.

Data Stations

Data stations in libraries are a unique way to present library instruction. As educators we realize that students have to have basic information before they can analyze, synthesize, or make predictions. Using the library data stations is an excellent way to obtain this basic information.

General or *basic information* is found in every resource. It is the easiest type of information for the student to find. They can go to dictionaries, encyclopedias, newspapers, magazines, television, and videos to find basic information. Once they have this basic information, they must utilize it.

The next step is *investigative information.* The student will have to look at several sources and analyze information and be discriminative. He will have to compare sources and draw inferences about the ones that meet his objective. This *investigative process* will take longer and time allotment should be considered by the instructor. During the planning stages, the teacher and librarian need to consider the time element.

The next step is synthesizing or *predicting outcomes.* Students must decide what to do with this information. Do they use it only for a written paper to hand in for a grade? Do they apply it to themselves and the environment? Can they predict educational outcomes based on this information? The instructor and librarian should consider this in the planning. The educational objective should go further than finding who is the leader of Iran; the students should ask themselves how the leader got there, and why this information would be of value to students.

Predicting outcomes is a skill that some students have mastered. Most students, however, need to be assisted in this process. If teachers and librarians plan for this additional skill in their original library activities, an increase in the student's ability to make judgments may become evident.

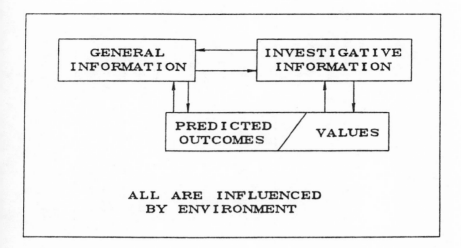

Students may reach a higher level in their thinking process which will hopefully project across the curriculum.

Library data stations can also give the student a chance to respond to his learning style. The many different instructional media and methods within the center give the student an opportunity to experience first-hand all the types of resources which are available. Students working in small groups will have the opportunity and freedom to ask questions that they might otherwise not have asked a teacher or librarian. They have the chance to choose how they learn best. The stations provide experiences which promote tactual, kinesthetic, auditory, and visual learning styles.

The following criteria should be met for each data station:

1. Each station will have an explanation that is visual and clear to the student.

2. Each station will have an activity which the student or user must physically touch.

3. Each station should be easy to use without requiring an instructor.

4. Each station should promote the individual student's learning style.

5. Each station should be a vital part of the library or media station.

6. Each station should promote the educational objective of the instructor and should assist the transfer of knowledge.

Library integrated data stations can be used to motivate the students to acquaint themselves with basic library skills at their individual pace and interest. The classroom teacher and librarian should work together to divide the students into groups according to their various academic levels, personalities, and leadership abilities.

A library can have as many data stations as the teacher and librarian need. The stations could include vertical files, the card catalog, a reference

	Day 1 or Monday	Day 2 or Tuesday	Day 3 or Wednesday	Day 4 or Thursday	Day 5 or Friday
Group #1	Initial Search	Microfiche Reference	SIRS Vertical Files	Computers Readers' Guide	CD-ROM Biography
Group #2	Initial Search	Reference SIRS	Vertical Files Computers	Readers' Guide CD-ROM	Biography Text on Microfiche
Group #3	Initial Search	SIRS Vertical Files	Computers Readers' Guide	CD-ROM Biography	Text on Microfiche Reference
Group #4	Initial Search	Vertical Files Computers	Readers' Guide CD-ROM	Biography Text on Microfiche	Reference SIRS
Group #5	Initial Search	Computers Readers' Guide	CD-ROM Biography	Text on Microfiche Reference	SIRS Vertical Files
Group #6	Initial Search	Readers' Guide CD-ROM	Biography Text on Microfiche	Reference SIRS	Vertical Files Computers
Group #7	Initial Search	CD-ROM Biography	Text on Microfiche Reference	SIRS Vertical Files	Computers Readers' Guide
Group #8	Initial Search	Biography Text on Microfiche	Reference SIRS	Vertical Files Computers	Readers' Guide CD-ROM

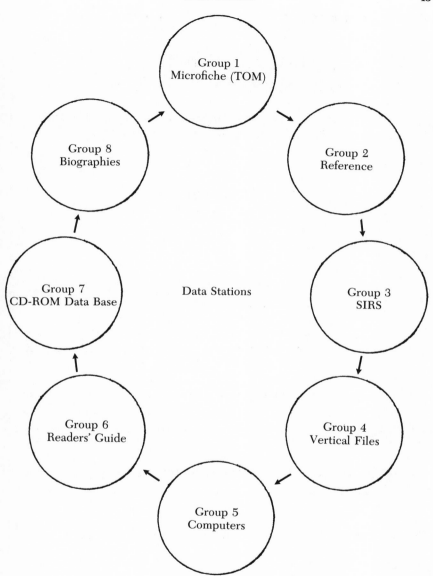

Data Stations

station, text on microfiche, the *Readers' Guide to Periodical Literature,* CD-ROM databases, computers, indexes, biographies, videos, and any other prescribed library "stations" that the teacher and students may need.

The librarian and teacher may want to evaluate the following Data Station Activity Sheets and choose the stations that they would like to emphasize. You may add or delete stations according to academic levels,

Text on Microfiche
Data Station Activity Sheet

Text on Microfiche is a current index with bibliographic reference from over 100 periodicals. The full text is on microfiche.

Directions

Visit the microfiche index.

1. How is the index arranged?_____

   _____

2. Choose a subject of interest. _____

3. Write the name of a magazine in which you could find information on that subject. _____

   _____

4. Write the date and page numbers for that magazine.

   _____

5. Do you like to use the text on microfiche? _____

6. Why is it important for you to be able to utilize library media, like text on microfiche? _____

   _____

Reference

World Almanacs and Yearbook Data Station Activity Sheet

Almanacs and yearbooks provide statistical and current information on a wide range of subjects.

Directions

Find an almanac or yearbook in the reference room and answer the following questions.

1. Who was the twenty-first president of the U.S.?

   _____

2. What is the population of the U.S.? _____

3. Who is the leader of Pakistan? _____

4. Name the largest body of water in the world. _____

   _____

5. Under the topic "government officials," who would become president if the president and vice president of the U.S. were assassinated?

   _____

Reference

Webster's Biographical Dictionary
Data Station Activity Sheet

Webster's Biographical Dictionary gives a brief description of a famous person, his background, and his contributions. These specific dictionaries are found in the reference area.

Directions

1. Find information on a famous person and tell why you think he or she was chosen to be in the dictionary.

   _____

   _____

   _____

2. How is this dictionary arranged?   _____

   _____

3. Look up the current president of the U.S. Were you able to find him in this resource? Why or why not?

   _____

   _____

   _____

Reference

Twentieth Century Authors
Data Station Activity Sheet

Twentieth Century Authors provides information about famous authors who lived in the twentieth century. This book will help the student with literary research on famous authors.

Directions

1. Find a favorite author and give the dates of birth and death.
   Name: _____
   Birth: _____ Death: _____

2. Name one literary contribution from this author._____
   _____

3. Name the nationality of this specific author. _____
   _____

4. What was a recurring theme or subject that this author wrote about? _____
   _____

5. How can you relate this author's works or ideas to your own life?
   _____
   _____
   _____

Reference

Encyclopedias
Data Station Activity Sheet

Encyclopedias give background information on a variety of topics. These reference books will be arranged in volumes and found in the reference area of the library.

Directions

1. List the names of the general encyclopedias which are in the reference area. _____
   _____
   _____
   _____

2. Choose one encyclopedia and describe what type of information you can find from it.
   Name of encyclopedia: _____
   Type of information: _____

3. Choose a topic that is interesting to you. Find that topic in the encyclopedia, name the topic, and write a brief summary of the article.
   Topic: _____
   Summary: _____
   _____
   _____

4. Why would a person your age find this topic interesting? Explain.
   _____

The SIRS Series
Data Station Activity Sheet

The SIRS Series is designed to provide timely information to a wide range of people from teenagers to senior citizens. The program consists of titles in loose-leaf volumes. Each volume contains carefully selected articles, reprinted in their entirety. The information has been printed in magazines and newspapers.

Directions

Choose a volume of the SIRS Series and answer the following questions.

1. What is the subject on your volume? _____

2. Does this volume have an index? _____

3. Choose a subject of interest in the index and write the entries and page numbers for that subject. _____
_____
_____

4. Write the bibliographic information from your article.
   a. Author _____
   b. Subject _____
   c. Date _____ Page # _____

5. Predict why or how this subject will be important to future generations. _____
_____

Vertical Files
Data Station Activity Sheet

The vertical files are files of information in alphabetical order. The files can be used for research purposes. Also check to see if your library has information on computer software. In some libraries these may be called information files.

Directions

Choose a topic of interest and locate the folder in the file cabinet.

1. Write something of interest from the folder about the subject and provide the following information:
Title of article: _____

2. Write a brief summary of an article from the folder.
   _____
   _____
   _____
   _____

3. Evaluate the vertical file and discuss how you could use this source for a health report.
   _____
   _____

4. Find an article on abortion, air pollution, robotics, or Adolph Hitler. Read one article and explain how this topic has affected the lives of millions of people.
   _____
   _____
   _____

Computers
Data Station Activity Sheet

Many types of informational and instructional software are available today. Computers are another method of furnishing students with information. Each school may have different software for different purposes.

1. Visit the computer station.

2. Choose and evaluate a subject of your choice.

3. Name the title of the software. _____

4. How could you use this information? _____

5. Find and go through a Word Processing program. How could you use this word processor with your school work? _____
_____
_____

Readers' Guide to Periodical Literature Data Station Activity Sheet

The *Readers' Guide to Periodical Literature*, a well-known and widely used index, contains a list of periodical articles arranged in alphabetical order by subject and author. The *Readers' Guide* indexes over 180 popular periodicals, or magazines, such as *Newsweek, Cosmopolitan, Sports Illustrated,* and *Psychology Today.* If looking for an article on a topic currently in the news, popular opinion, or the layman's approach to a topic, this index will be most helpful.

Common abbreviations

il—illustrations
ed—editor, edited, edition
q—quarterly
abr—abridged
bi-w—biweekly
cont—continued

Month abbreviations

Ja—January	Ju—July
F—February	Ag—August
Mr—March	S—September
Ap—April	O—October
My—May	N—November
Je—June	D—December

Bird of Happiness.   R. Wilder.   il Sci Dig 91:112 + F '83
Science Digest volume 91 pages 112 + February 1983

Directions

Read the example of a citation above and answer the following questions.

1. Write the title of the magazine: _____

2. Write the author of the article:_____

3. Write the name of the article: _____

4. Write the volume number, date, and page number:_____

5. Find a citation in the *Readers' Guide* which could help you get information for your future occupation. Write a summary or synopsis of the article.
   _____
   _____
   _____

CD-ROM Database
Data Station Activity Sheet

CD-ROM is a new storage medium on a laser disk that can serve as a quick, economical source of information for students, researchers, writers, and professionals across the curriculum. *Grolier Encyclopedia* is one of the most popular products on CD-ROM, which is found in the reference area.

Humanities Index, Readers' Guide to Periodical Literature, Business Periodicals Index, Applied Science and Technology Index, and *ERIC* are a few of the available databases that will aid the research student.

Directions

1. Visit the CD-ROM station and become acquainted with the available databases. Check the databases that are available at this station.

   _____*Applied Science and Technology*
   _____*Grolier Encyclopedia*
   _____*PC Globe*
   _____*World Almanac*
   _____*Bartlett's Familiar Quotations*
   _____*Readers' Guide to Periodical Literature*

2. Choose a database that interests you and tell how you could use this information. _____
   _____

3. Did you get help from a library staff member?
   Yes_____ No_____

4. Find an article or information pertinent to the year 2000. Summarize the article. _____
   _____

Biographies
Data Station Activity Sheet

Biographies are books about famous people. All biographies may be located in a specific place in the library.

Directions

Choose a biography of your choice and answer the following questions.

1. Name: _____

2. Date of birth: _____

3. Date of death: _____

4. Contribution to society: _____
   _____
   _____

5. Call #: _____

6. If he or she had lived today, predict how he or she would have felt about the national debt. Explain: _____
   _____

educational objectives, and resource availability. These activities can also be used with college students on an independent basis.

The data stations consist of activity folders which are placed near the resources being studied. For example, the activity folder for SIRS would be placed by the SIRS material in the library, thus becoming the SIRS Data Station. The teacher or librarian should make one copy per student of the data station activity sheets. The class should be divided into groups of 3 to 5 students. Each group will begin this activity at a different station and rotate in a clockwise manner until all of the stations are completed. A folder in which to put completed work will be available at each station.

Charades

Playing charades is an interesting, stimulating, and educational way to culminate orientation. Students of all ages enjoy playing games, and charades is a classic. This activity allows students the opportunity to review strategic library terminology while being creative and having fun.

The goal is for the group to guess the word or phrase the presenter is trying to act out. In this specific Charades game, the purpose is for the students to guess words or phrases related to the Library.

Rules for playing Orientation Charades are:

1. Two groups of approximately 15 students.

2. Choose the first presenter. The person who correctly identifies the word or phrase will become the next presenter. Continue in this manner throughout the game.

3. No pointing, no spelling out words, no talking, and no props.

4. To show how many words, hold up that many fingers.

5. To show how many syllables, put that many fingers on your forearm.

6. To show that a word sounds like another word, point at your ear.

7. The student who guesses correctly must either define the word or phrase, or give pertinent information about it. Example: bibliography means a list of sources.

8. The teacher may have to be the referee. The teacher can assign a student to act as referee if she wishes.

9. The group that guesses the most correct terms wins the game. The prize for winning might be to get to leave class first, to get the next set of papers back first, to get to sit where they want for a day or week, or go to the library for pleasure reading for a day. Any number of options could be used as a reward.

Following is a list of words and phrases that relate directly or indirectly to the library. The teacher needs to make two lists of these words — one for each group. The words or phrases should be cut up into strips, folded, and placed in a container (box, jar, hat, etc.), so the Charades presenter can draw out a topic from the folded pieces of paper and act it out.

This game can be used with: book titles, authors' names, historical and current events, science terminology, or with any other discipline. It involves dramatics, speaking and listening skills, social intervention, leadership enhancement, and teamwork.

Charades Topics

Vertical Files	SIRS
Encyclopedia	Fiction
Biographies	Independent User
Read for Fun	Page
Non-Fiction	Research
Indexes	Stay on Task
Twentieth Century Authors	Autobiography
Readers' Guide	Text on Microfiche
Bibliographies	Learning Styles
Phrases	Call Number
Periodical	Reference Section
Magazine	Dictionary
Teacher	Copyright Date
World Almanac	Dewey Decimal System
Subject Heading	Classification System
Topic	Circulation Desk
Search	Stacks
John F. Kennedy	Sizzling Sixties
Jimi Hendrix	Martin Luther King
James Dean	Elvis Presley
Ernest Hemingway	Marilyn Monroe
Arthur Miller	John Steinbeck
Librarian	Student
Card Catalog	Team

Bibliography

ALA Handbook of Organization, 1981/1982. Chicago: American Library Association, 1981.
Apple Software Directory. PC Telemart/Vanloves, 1984.
The Audio-Visual Equipment Directory. Nat'l Audio-Visual Association, Inc., 1982.

AV Cataloguing and Processing Simplified. Audiovisual Catalogers, Inc., 1971.
Behavior Management in the School Library Media Center. American Library Association, 1985.
Bilingual Educational Publications in Print 1983. New York, NY: R. R. Bowker, 1983.
Brigham, Nancy. *How to Do Leaflets, Newsletters and Newspapers.* New York, NY: Hastings House, 1982.
Broadus, Robert N. *Selecting Materials for Libraries.* H. W. Wilson, 1973.
Cory, Emmett. *Grants for Libraries.* Littleton, CO: Libraries Unlimited, 1982.
Costa, Betty. *A Micro Handbook for Small Libraries and Media Centers.* Littleton, CO: Libraries Unlimited, Inc., 1983.
Davies, Ruth Ann. *The School Library.* New York: R.R. Bowker, 1969.
_____. *The School Library Media Center.* New York: R. R. Bowker, 1974.
_____. *The School Library Media Program.* 3d ed. New York: R. R. Bowker, 1979.
Davis, Harold S., ed. *Instructional Media Center.* Bloomington: Indiana University Press, 1971.
Drazan, Joseph Gerald. *An Annotated Bibliography of Eric Bibliographies, 1966–1980.* Westport, CT: Greenwood, 1982.
Durnin, Richard G. *American Education.* Detroit, MI: Gale Research Company, 1982.
Educational Film/Video Locator. (2 volumes). 3d ed. New York: R. R. Bowker, 1986.
Ewald, William R. *100 Short Films About the Human Environment.* Community Arts Association of Santa Barbara, Inc., 1982.
Foor, Ruth. *The Complete Book of Forms for Managing the School Library Media Center.* The Center for Applied Research in Education, Inc., 1982.
Fosdick, Howard. *Computer Basics for Librarians and Information Scientists.* Information Resource Press, 1981.
Gates, Jean Key. *Introduction to Librarianship.* New York: McGraw, 1968.
Gatti, Richard D., and Daniel J. Gatti. *Encyclopedic Dictionary of School Law.* Englewood Cliffs, NJ: Parker, 1975.
Green, Lee. *501 Ways to Use the Overhead Projector.* Libraries Unlimited, Inc., 1982.
Hoffman, Herbert H. *International Index to Recorded Poetry.* New York, NY: H. W. Wilson, 1983.
Instant Facts. Chicago: World Book Encyclopedia, 1983.
Instruction in School Library Media Center Use (K–12). 2d ed. Chicago: American Library Association, 1985.
Karpisek, Marian E. *Making Self-Teaching Kits for Library Skills.* Chicago: American Library Association, 1983.
Katz, Bill. *Magazines for School Libraries.* New York: R. R. Bowker, 1987.
Katz, William A. *Your Library.* Orlando, FL: Holt, Rinehart and Winston, 1984.
Kohn, Rita, and Krysta A. Tepper. *Have You Got What They Want?* Metuchen, NJ: Scarecrow, 1982.
Lane, Hana Umlauf, ed. *The World Almanac & Book of Facts, 1984.* Newspaper Enterprise, 1983.
Lapedes, Daniel N., ed. *McGraw-Hill Encyclopedia of Energy.* McGraw, 1976.
Library of Congress. *Films and Other Materials for Projection.* Washington, 1976, 1978.
Lushington, Nolan. *Libraries Designed for Users.* Gaylord Professional Publications, 1979.
Mallet, Jerry J. *Library Skills Activities Kit.* The Center for Applied Research in Education, 1981.

Marra, Jean M., ed. *Abridged Readers' Guide to Periodical Literature.* Bronx, NY: H. W. Wilson, 1981.

National Geographic Index, 1947–1983. Washington, DC: National Geographic Society, 1984.

Nordling, Jo Anne. *Dear Faculty.* Faxon, 1976.

Parks, A. Lee, and Marilyn K. Rousseau. *The Public Law Supporting Mainstreaming.* Learning Concepts, 1977.

Periodicals for School Libraries. Rev. ed. Chicago: American Library Association, 1973.

Peterson, Carolyn Sue. *Reference Books for Young Readers.* New York: R. R. Bowker, 1988.

Roberts, Anne F. *Library Instruction for Librarians.* Littleton, CO: Libraries Unlimited, Inc., 1982.

Schmid, William T. *Media Center Management.* New York: Hastings House, 1980.

School Library Media Annual 1983. Littleton, CO: Libraries Unlimited, Inc., 1983.

Sheehy, Eugene Paul. *Guide to Reference Books.* 9th ed. Chicago: American Library Association, 1976.

Silverman, Eleanor. *One Hundred and One Media Center Ideas.* Scarecrow, Inc., 1980.

Slote, Stanley J. *Weeding Library Collections.* Littleton, CO: Libraries Unlimited, 1975.

Smallwood, Carol. *Exceptional Free Library Resource Materials.* Littleton, CO: Libraries Unlimited, 1984.

Tables and Formulas. World Book Encyclopedia, Inc., 1983.

Twaite, James A. *Introductory Statistics.* Glenview, IL: Scott, Foresman and Company, 1979.

Van Vliet, Lucille W. *Media Skills for Middle Schools.* Littleton, CO: Libraries Unlimited, 1984.

Walker, H. Thomas. *Teaching Media Skills.* Littleton, CO: Libraries Unlimited, Inc., 1982.

Warner, Alice Sizer, and Elizabeth Bole Eddison. *Volunteers in Libraries.* New York: R. R. Bowker, 1977.

Weins, Jean Riddle. *Nonbook Material.* 1st ed. Ottawa, ON: Canadian Library Association, 1973.

Whaley, Nita B. *School Volunteers.* National School Public Relations Association, 1973.

Wolff, Kathryn. *The Best Science Films, Filmstrips, and Videocassettes for Children.* Washington, DC: American Association for the Advancement of Science, 1982.

Woods, Lawrence A. *The Librarian's Guide to Microcomputer Technology and Applications.* American Society for Information Science, 1983.

Wynar, Christine Gehrt. *Guide to Reference Books for School Media Centers.* Littleton, CO: Libraries Unlimited, Inc., 1981.

Wynar, Christine L. *Guide to Reference Books for School Media Centers.* Littleton, CO: Libraries Unlimited, 1973.

II. Reading Taxonomy

Reading is thinking. It is the key to student achievement. Most educators agree that reading is the basic component for success across the curriculum.

Reading can be a wonderful experience for young adults. A person has an emotional experience when he becomes involved with the written symbols we call words. Senses are touched; pictures are painted; voices are heard.

Realistically, formal reading instruction rarely occurs after elementary school. Therefore, if a student is not a proficient reader by completion of the elementary years, his chance of being an independent reader in secondary school may be nonexistent. Reading should be formally encouraged throughout high school and college. Educators need to emphasize that reading is the single most important skill that will prepare students for college and lifetime learning.

Many people are illiterate because they lack the will to read. They depend upon electronic technology—television, radio, and videos—to interpret the culture. When a student is constantly bombarded with another person's interpretation of current events, science, literature, or history, the student does not have to analyze the situation himself. He does not have to think.

When a person reads about current events or reads a book, he has to analyze the data himself.

There is a growing concern that students in American high schools and colleges lack reading skills necessary for interpreting information. Standardized tests show that many students cannot translate and evaluate written information on the appropriate grade level.

Schools are spending more money and providing more individualized programs than ever before, but according to these standardized tests results, schools are not being successful. The educational community cannot take all the blame, however.

A teacher who is responsible for 150 students can only fulfill so many obligations. Parents and individual students must take more responsibility for their educational development, and they can do this by making reading a priority.

Schools should emphasize reading. Students should be encouraged to read more than the core curriculum requirements. They should be encouraged to read anything of interest: comics, romances, thrillers, books in series, classics, and newspapers. The more a student reads, the more discriminating he becomes. He becomes more aware of symbolism and sharpens his analytical thinking. Librarians and teachers can use numerous activities to incorporate and encourage these analytical thinking and reading skills.

Often the young adult selects his reading material because the subjects are unusual or controversial. Educators may be guilty of discouraging young adults from reading anything other than classic literature.

We are presenting a reading program which includes a variety of reading activities and reading lists appropriate for young adult and college students.

We chose ideas of high interest for this age group, ideas that are not introduced in traditional textbooks, but that are, nonetheless, academically challenging.

The classic character analysis provides opportunities for students to be exposed to traditional writing methods. Literary criticism teaches students to analyze several critical approaches to studying an author. The critical analysis encourages students to read several works by one author and scrutinize the author's intent by evaluating all elements of his literature. Also, the classic reading list provides an infinity of characters for students to enjoy.

Small group activity is the focus of the round table discussion. Students are given opportunities to talk about books and authors. Exposure to and application of such literary terms as theme, point of view, irony, and allusion encourage upper level thinking skills. The students utilize a critique which gives them a chance to evaluate their peers, as well as themselves. Other motivational reading activities are included in this section.

A school-wide endeavor involving reading is the Banned Book Club, which concentrates on classic literature that commonly appears on censorship lists.

The BBC provides opportunities for teachers, librarians, students, parents, and community leaders to discuss the banning of classic literature. Friends of the Library encourages parents, students, and patrons to become aware of the needs and benefits of the library.

Reading can be many things. It can be an escape from reality or a chance to gain new insights into life. It is a universal medium. All ages and walks of life can enjoy reading. Whether mystery, romance, or adventure, books have entirely new worlds to explore.

Reading Lists

Action

Cowboys

Sackett Louis Lamour
My Ántonia Willa Cather
Log of a Cowboy Andy Adams
Wait for Me, Watch for Me, Ella Bee Patricia Beaty
Soldier Girl Richard Boxing
Texas Trail Drive Warren Garet
Millie's Boy Robert Peck
The Brave Cowboy Edward Abbey
Pistol: A Novel Adrienne Richard
The Virginian Owen Wister

Indians

Bury My Heart at Wounded Knee Dee Brown
Showdown at Little Big Horn Dee Brown
Light in the Forest Conrad Richter
The Westerners Dee Brown
Fawn Robert Peck
The Western Allen Eyles
The Life and Death of Yellow Bird James Foreman
The Heritage of the Desert Zane Grey
When Legends Die Hal Borland
Death of Evening Star Jamake Highwater

Outlaws

The Youngers Fight for Freedom Warren C. Bronaugh
The Border Outlaws James William Buel
Charles W. Quantrell John C. Burch
Jesse James Was My Neighbor Homer Croy
Illustrated Lives and Adventures of Frank and Jesse James and the Younger Brothers: The Noted Western Outlaws Joseph Dacus
Outlaws on Horseback Harry S. Drago
The Bad Men of the West George Hendricks
Geronimo: His Own Story ed. S. M. Barrett
Bad Men of the West Robert Elman
The Outlaws: The Authentic Wild West James Horan

Adventure

Treasure Island Robert Lewis Stevenson
Island of the Blue Dolphins Scott O'Dell
The Black Pearl Scott O'Dell
Huckleberry Finn Mark Twain
Alive Piers Read
Gulliver's Travels Jonathan Swift
The Merry Adventures of Robin Hood Howard Pyle
Twenty Thousand Leagues Under the Sea Jules Verne
Around the World in Eighty Days Jules Verne
Lord of the Flies William Golding

Thrillers

Coma Robin Cook
The Asphalt Jungle W. R. Burnett

Tales of Mystery & Imagination
Edgar Allan Poe
Murder on the Orient Express
Agatha Christie
A Judgement in Stone Ruth
Rendell
The Green Ripper John D.
MacDonald
The Circular Staircase Mary
Roberts Rinehart
The Nursery Rhyme Murders
Agatha Christie
Murder Among Friends Elizabeth
Ferrars
RSVP Murder M. E. Everhart

Suspense

Death in a Tenured Position
Amanda Cross
The Dutch Shoe Mystery Ellery
Queen
The Young Unicorns Madeleine
L'Engle
Assignment: Suspense Helen
MacInnes
A Death in the Life Dorothy S.
Davis
Policewoman Dorothy Uhnak
Laidlaw William McIlvanney
The Postman Always Rings Twice
James Cain
Clairvoyant Countess Dorothy
Gilman
A Thief of Time Tony Hillerman

Espionage

Murder on the Orient Express
Agatha Christie
The Circular Staircase Mary
Roberts Rhinehart
The Innocence of Father Brown
G. K. Chesterton

The Mystery of Edwin Drood
Charles Dickens
The Assassination Bureau Jack
London
The Investigation Dorothy Whrak
The Maltese Falcon Dashiell
Hammett
Majestic Whitley Strieber
I Led Three Lives Herbert Phil-
brick
Spies and Spymasters Jock Haswell

Sleuth

*The Adventures of Sherlock
Holmes* Arthur Conan Doyle
Tales of Terror and Mystery
Arthur Conan Doyle
Sleeping Murder Agatha Christie
A Chubbale Woman Reginald Hill
Died on a Rainy Sunday Joan
Aiken
The Moonstone Wilkie Collins
A False Inspector Peter Lovesey
The Midnight Raymond Chandler
Forgery Phyllis Bentley
The Skeleton Man Jay Bennett

Supernatural

Ghost/Horror

Pet Sematary Stephen King
Summer of Fear Lois Duncan
Witchcraft in America Clifford
Alderman
It Stephen King
The Turn of the Screw Henry
James
The Witch Mary Johnston
Nancy Drew Ghost Stories
Carolyn Keene

Grendel John Gardner
The Complete Ghost Stories of Charles Dickens Charles Dickens
The Toy Cemetery William Johnston

Gothic Horror

Vathele William Beckford
Frankenstein Mary Shelley
Fall of the House of Usher Edgar Allan Poe
Rebecca Daphne Du Maurier
The Castle of Otranto Horace Walpole
The Mysteries of Udolpho Ann Radcliffe
The Monk Matthew Lewis
Gothic Tales of Terror Peter Haining
Ladies of Horror Seon Manley and Gogo Lewis
The Old English Baron Clara Reeves

Mythology

Mythology Edith Hamilton
Bulfinch's Mythology Thomas Bulfinch
Stars in Our Heaven Peter Lum
The Greek Way Edith Hamilton
Antigone Sophocles
Oedipus Rex Sophocles
The Cyclops Bernard Euslin
The Golden Fleece and the Heroes Who Lived Before Achilles Colum Padraic
Clash of the Titans Alan Dean Foster
Iliad, or *Odyssey* Homer

Sci/Fi — Fantasy

Foundation Isaac Asimov
The Dispossessed Ursula Le Guin
The City and the Stars Arthur Clark
Friday Robert Heinlein
The War of the Worlds H. G. Wells
Out of the Silent Planet C. S. Lewis
The Ship Who Sang Anne McCaffrey
Watership Down Richard Adams
The Fellowship of the Ring J. R. R. Tolkien

Romance

Historical

Green Mansions William Henry Hudson
Mistress of Mellyn Victoria Holt
Anna Karenina Leo Tolstoy
Ivanhoe Sir Walter Scott
Ethan Frome Edith Wharton
The Age of Innocence Edith Wharton
Gone with the Wind Margaret Mitchell
Little Women Louisa May Alcott
Little Men Louisa May Alcott
To Have and to Hold Mary Johnston

Gothic

Jane Eyre Charlotte Brontë
Pride and Prejudice Jane Austen
Wuthering Heights Emily Brontë
The Curse of Clifton Emma Southworth
Mistress of Mellyn Victoria Holt

The Castle of Otranto Horace Walpole

St. Elmo, Augusta Jane Evans Wilson

Amelia Sally Wood

The Asylum Isaac Mitchell

Charlotte Temple Susanna Haswell Rowson

Modern

Love Story Erich Segal

The Thornbirds Colleen McCullough

Love Is Eternal Irving Stone

The President's Lady Irving Stone

Till We Meet Again Judith Krantz

The Love Letters of Timothy Owens Constance Green

The Year Summer Died Patricia Lee Gauch

When We First Met Norma Fox Mazer

Roses Barbara Cohen

Young Adults

And Both Were Young Madeleine L'Engle

Camilla Madeleine L'Engle

Someone to Love Norma F. Mazer

Up a Road Slowly Irene Hunt

Close Enough to Touch Richard Peck

Seventeenth Summer Maureen Daly

To Tell Your Love Mary Stolz

A Girl Can Dream Betty Cavanna

Goodnight, Gracie Julie Reece Deaver

The Fat Girl Marilyn Sachs

Human Interest

Animals

All Things Bright and Beautiful James Herriot

Old Yeller Fred Gipson

Big Red Jim Kjelgaard

Call of the Wild Jack London

Moby Dick Herman Melville

The Yearling Marjorie Rawlings

Where the Red Fern Grows Wilson Rawls

Sounder William Armstrong

Then There Were None Charles Roth

Summer of the Monkey Wilson Rawls

Family/Friendship

Rich in Love Josephine Humphreys

The Beautiful and the Damned F. Scott Fitzgerald

A Separate Peace John Knowles

Rumblefish S. E. Hinton

The Chosen Chaim Potok

Headman Kin Platt

Tiger Eyes Judy Blume

Where the Lilies Bloom Vera Cleaver and Bill Cleaver

Home Before Dark Sue Ellen Bridgers

Death Be Not Proud John Gunther

Social Problems

Bridge to Terabirthia Katherine Patterson

Pigman Paul Zindel

Catcher in the Rye J. D. Salinger

Chocolate War Robert Cormier

Fahrenheit 451 Ray Bradbury

Outsiders S. E. Hinton
To Kill a Mockingbird Harper Lee
The Man Without a Face Isabelle Holland
Mr. and Mrs. Bo Jo Jones Ann Head
Deathwatch Robb White

Humor

Funny People Steve Allen
The Cat Ate My Gymsuit Paula Danziger
Nobody's Perfect Donald Westlake
The Thurber Carnival James Thurber
Happy to Be Here Garrison Keillor
If I Love You, Am I Trapped Forever? M. E. Kerr
The Dog Days of Arthur Cane J. Ernesto Bethancourt
SUDS Judie Angell
It Can't Be Helped Benjamin Lee
My Darling, My Hamburger Paul Zindel

Ethics

Religion/Philosophy

Illusions Richard Bach
Lilies of the Field William Barrett
I Heard the Owl Call My Name Margaret Craven
The Robe Lloyd Douglas
Two from Galilee Marjorie Holmes
Joni Joni Eareckson
Exodus Leon Uris
The Holy Bible
Bronze Bow Elizabeth Speare
The Prophet Kahlil Gibran

Politics

Looking Backward Edward Bellamy
The Jungle Upton Sinclair
The Count of Monte Cristo Alexandre Dumas
Crime and Punishment Fyodor Dostoevsky
Republic Plato
Miracle of Philadelphia Catherine Bowen
Silent Spring Rachel Carson
All the King's Men Robert Penn Warren
Unbought and Unbossed Shirley Jackson
A Tale of Two Cities Charles Dickens

Success/Money

How to Win Friends and Influence People Dale Carnegie
Ask Beth Elizabeth Winship
The Great Gatsby F. Scott Fitzgerald
Barbarians at the Gate Bryan Burrough
The Rights of Young People Alan Sussman
Understanding of the Stock Market Janet Lou
Getting It Together Robert Ewen
Hotline Margaret Hyde
You Are Somebody Special Charlie Shedd
Free to Choose Joyce Mitchell

Personal Experience

Black Like Me John Griffin
A Walk Across America Peter Jenkins

A Night to Remember Linda
  Walker
*Zen and the Art of Motorcycle
  Maintenance* Robert Pirsig
Colonies in Space Frederic
  Golden
Body Language Julius Fast
A Christmas Carol Charles
  Dickens
Yes, I Can Sammy Davis, Jr.
*The Diary of a New England
  Whaler* Leonard Everett Fisher
Confessions of Nat Turner William
  Styron

Minorities

Orientals

The Good Earth Pearl S. Buck
Child of the Owl Laurence Yep
Henny Kamuru Betty Cavanaugh
Burma Rifles Frank Bonham
Stories of Hawaii Jack London
Hawaii James Michener
A Mountain of Gold Max Evans
A Thousand Cranes Yasunari
  Kawabata
Fifth Chinese Daughter Jade
  Wong
East Meets West George Goldberg

Afro/Blacks

Roots Alex Haley
Invisible Man Ralph Ellison
Native Son Richard Wright
Autobiography of Malcolm X
  Malcolm X
To Be a Slave Julius Lester
*The Life and Words of Martin
  Luther* Ira Peck Lang, Jr.
Roll of Thunder, Hear My Cry

Mildred Taylor
Sounder William Armstrong
I Know Why the Caged Bird Sings
  Maya Angelou
Beloved Toni Morrison

Women

Diary of Anne Frank Frances
  Goodrich & Albert Hackett
The Color Purple Alice Walker
Susan B. Anthony Iris Noble
Ten Brave Women Sonia
  Daugherty
*Lady for the Defense: A Biography
  of Belva Lockwood* Mary Fox
The Silent Storm Marion Brown &
  Ruth Crone
Whatever Happened to Amelia?
  Melinda Blau
My Appalachia Rebecca Caudill
*I Touch the Future: The Story of
  Christa McAuliffe* Robert
  Hohler
True Grit Charles Portis

Spanish/Latin

West Side Story Leonard Bern-
  stein
The Nation Thief Robert Houston
In Praise of the Stepmother Vargas
  Llosa
This Is Espie Sanchez Terry
  Dunnahoo
*The Autobiography of Brown
  Buffalo* Oscar Acosta
Heart of Aztlan Rudolfo Anaya
My Heart Lies South Elizabeth B.
  Trevino
South by Southwest John Tebbel
  and Ramon Ruiz
The Bridge of San Luis Rey Thorn-
  ton Wilder

And Now Miguel Joseph Krumgold

War

Modern Wars

1984 H. G. Wells
Andromeda Strain Michael Crichton
Hunt for Red October Tom Clancy
The Cambodia File Jack Anderson
Vietnam: A History Stanley Karnov
Children of the Dust
Park's Quest, Katherine Paterson
Winners and Losers Gloria Emerson
A Soldier's Story Omar Bradley
Away All Boats Kenneth Dodson

World Wars

Hiroshima John Hersey
Iwo Jima John Hersey
All Quiet on the Western Front Erich Maria Remarque
The Sun Also Rises Ernest Hemingway
Summer of My German Soldier Bette Greene
Rise and Fall of Adolph Hitler William Shirer
Last Nine Days of the Bismarck C. S. Forester
The Visit T. Degens
The Investigation Peter Weiss
Day of Infamy Walter Lord

Civil War

Gone with the Wind Margaret Mitchell
The Tall Woman Wilma Dykeman
Across Five Aprils Irene Hunt
To Appomattox Burke Davis
The Red Badge of Courage Stephen Crane
Marching On Jane Boyd
North and South John Jakes
Spies for the Blue and Gray Harnett Kane
Mosby, Gray Ghost of the Confederacy Jonathan Daniels
The Rules of the Riot James Bond

Revolutions

Dr. Zhivago Boris Pasternak
The Story of Phillis Wheatley: The Poetess of the American Revolution Shirley Graham
War and Peace Leo Tolstoy
Sea Captain from Salem Leonard Wibberley
Men Who Made the Nation John R. Dos Passos
The Federalist Era John C. Miller
Wilderness Clearing Walter Edmonds
Drums Along the Mohawk Walter Edmonds
Jersey Rebel Kensil Bell
The Big Knives Bruce Lancaster

Classic Character Analysis

A character analysis can be utilized with any type of reading: fiction, non-fiction, biographies, short stories. A character analysis may be of any length. We would like to suggest a five paragraph composition in which every paragraph contains at least five good sentences.

The student will choose a person from his reading, preferably a character that he especially liked or disliked.

The first paragraph should be called the introductory paragraph and must include a thesis statement in which three traits or characteristics of the certain person or character are presented. The thesis statement is a one sentence statement that the three body paragraphs will refer back to.

The body of the character analysis will include the second, third, and fourth paragraphs of the paper. Each of these paragraphs will refer back to a specific characteristic mentioned in the thesis statement. Each paragraph must also include a direct quote from the book or story that substantiates the characteristic being discussed in that paragraph.

The concluding paragraph should draw the paper together. In this paragraph, the thesis statement should be restated and the paper summed up.

Students should deliberately try to use sentence variety. They should also be conscious of the transition from one paragraph to another. The paragraphs should flow easily from one subject to the next.

Some possible methods for writing a character analysis can be as follows:

1. Showing main characteristics, like generosity, lovingness, gentility, maliciousness.

2. Showing the development or change of a character: traits possessed at the beginning, middle, and end of book; how did the character change?

3. Showing principal or main incidents as they relate and bring out the character that is being discussed.

Classic Book List

Pride and Prejudice Jane Austen
Go Tell It on the Mountain James Baldwin
Père Goriot Honoré de Balzac
The Lilies of the Field William E. Barrett
Jane Eyre Charlotte Brontë
Wuthering Heights Emily Brontë
The Good Earth Pearl Buck
The Pilgrim's Progress John Bunyan
The Way of All Flesh Samuel Butler
Alice's Adventures in Wonderland Lewis Carroll

Don Quixote Miguel de Cervantes (Saavedra)
The Cherry Orchard Anton Pavlovich Chekhov
The Last of the Mohicans James Fenimore Cooper
The Open Boat and Other Stories Stephen Crane
The Red Badge of Courage Stephen Crane
The Divine Comedy Dante
The Brothers Karamazov Fyodor Dostoevsky
Crime and Punishment Fyodor Dostoevsky

Character Analysis
Startup Form

1. Name of your character:

2. Book:

3. Three characteristics:
   A.
   B.
   C.

4. Put these three characteristics together to form a thesis statement (one sentence).

5. Put questions 1, 2, and 4 together, along with general statements (central ideas) that should run throughout the paper, to form the first paragraph.

6. Find three quotes from the book that prove or show the three characteristics from the thesis statement.
   A.
   B.
   C.

The Count of Monte Cristo Alexandre Dumas
Medea Euripides
Invisible Man Ralph Ellison
Madame Bovary Gustave Flaubert
The Prophet Kahlil Gibran
Mythology Edith Hamilton
The Greek Way Edith Hamilton
The House of the Seven Gables Nathaniel Hawthorne
The Scarlet Letter Nathaniel Hawthorne
Iliad Homer
The Rise of Silas Lapham William Dean Howells
The American Henry James
The Portrait of a Lady Henry James
The Rubaiyat Omar Khayyam
The Sea Wolf Jack London
Billy Budd Herman Melville
Moby Dick Herman Melville

The Modern King James Version of the Holy Bible Teenage version, Green, ed.
The Octopus Frank Norris
Short Stories Edgar Allan Poe
The Jungle Upton Sinclair
Uncle Tom's Cabin Harriet Beecher Stowe
Walden Henry David Thoreau
Anna Karenina Count Leo Tolstoy
War and Peace Count Leo Tolstoy
Candide Voltaire
The Adventures of Tom Sawyer Mark Twain
The Adventures of Huckleberry Finn Mark Twain
A Connecticut Yankee in King Arthur's Court Mark Twain
Ethan Frome Edith Wharton
The Age of Innocence Edith N. J. Wharton
Our Town Thornton Wilder

Literary Criticism

A literary criticism is the evaluation of literature. This analysis of the author's intent includes several classifications which are moralistic, impressionistic, biographical, historical, psychological, archetypal, or formalist. These different approaches are all concerned with elements which reveal the range of possible bases for the act of critical judgment.

The moralistic approach is concerned with the author's intent to present a moral vision of reality.

The impressionistic approach involves the critic's personal response to a literary work. An example is a critic who attempts to explain and analyze pleasurable sensations. The biographical approach assumes that by examining the facts and motive of an author's life, the critic can understand the author's intent or meaning. The historical approach connects the literary work as a product of its social heritage. Historical critics may connect literature with a social force.

The psychological approach deals with the interpretation and personality of characterization. The archetypal approach involves an analysis of universal patterns in a character such as James Dean in *The Rebel*

Without a Cause. Last is the formalist approach which stresses the linguistic texture of the message. This approach is concerned with the structure of irony, tone, etc., and not the message.

The teacher can dress strangely or can act strangely by dropping books, talking about unrelated subjects in front of the class, etc. When the "strange" educator leaves, the librarian can ask the class what is wrong with the teacher. The students and librarian can criticize the teacher. This can present an excellent opportunity to define literary criticism.

The librarian could also have material which deals with literary criticism. The students (in groups) will have an opportunity to review and study criticism material on their favorite author. This group activity will promote collaborative learning. After the students feel comfortable and familiar with an author's style, characteristics, etc., they can select a spokesperson to represent them to the class.

One activity which the students can do is called "Who Am I?". Each group representative can give the class specific literary information about their author. The class should then guess who is being represented.

Example: I am a witty, humorous author who loves to write about the winding Mississippi. "I've spent more time yawning than I have doing manual labor." A favorite pal of mine is Tom Sawyer. Who am I?

The literary criticism experience is one in which students are involved on a regular basis. They recommend books to teachers, classmates, parents, and relatives. They discuss why they liked the book or author. Students are literary critics; however, when an instructor begins to teach literary criticism, students may have a problem with the formality of the lesson.

Role playing can serve an instructional need when teaching literary criticism by presenting the material on an informal basis. Through role playing, the teacher and librarian can show how the word criticism can be misused.

There are many different sources about specific authors and specific literature. There are books of criticism as well as journals.

General indexes which can be helpful in literary research are:

Readers' Guide to Periodical Literature
Humanities Index

Social Sciences Index
MLA International Bibliography

These lists of sources and bibliographies of criticism may also be helpful:

American and British Poetry: A Guide to the Criticism, 1925–1978

Index to Criticisms of British and American Poetry
Poetry Explication

Short Fiction Criticism
Twentieth-Century Short Story
  Explication
American Short-Fiction Criticism
  and Scholarship, 1959–1977
American Novel: A Checklist of
  Twentieth Century Criticism
The English Novel, 1578–1956: A

Checklist of Twentieth Century
  Criticisms
English Novel Explication: Criti-
  cisms to 1972
The English Novel: Twentieth Cen-
  tury Criticism
American Drama Criticism

Gale Research Company publishes selected reference sets which cover different time periods:

Literature Criticism from 1400 to
  1800
Shakespearean Criticism
Nineteenth-Century Literature
  Criticism
Twentieth-Century Literary

Criticism (authors who died
from 1900 to 1960)
Contemporary Literary Criticism
(authors now living or who died
after December 31, 1959)

Literary Analysis

A literary analysis is a more complex critical endeavor in which each student will

1. Read at least three major works (short stories, poetry collections, essays, novels) written by the same author.

2. Compile background information and criticism about the author and his works.

3. Organize ideas into a paper.
   A. Recurring themes
   B. Similar characters
   C. Autobiographical substance
   D. Similar type
   E. Comparison/contrast of characters or elements of an author's literature

4. Use proper documentation.
   A. Endnoting (MLA, APA, etc.)
   B. Footnoting

Round Table Discussion

A round table discussion is a critical evaluation, discussion, and group presentation about an author and his literature. The purpose in promoting a round table discussion is to encourage reading. This is a type of collaborative learning in which students will read books written by the same author and develop an appreciation and understanding of that author's works.

Students are notoriously social creatures who enjoy group activities. Utilizing a round table discussion in which several students work together reading books by the same author or books about the same subject encourages critical thinking, interest, and motivation in reading.

By the time students reach secondary school, they are tired of book reports. Often, it is easier for them to "beat the system" by watching the movie or reading the Cliff Notes, instead of reading the book. They have no problem with completing the usual book report 'form' without reading the book. They can easily get a summary of most books from many sources.

When the student is not challenged, reading becomes a chore instead of a creative experience. Teachers and librarians need to consciously plan reading programs that will benefit students academically and that students will enjoy.

The following discussion is designed to promote growth and development in reading. It will also enhance social interaction, leadership opportunities, and critical thinking skills. This discussion has been implemented in a secondary setting with overwhelming success motivating young adults to read independently. Students challenge each other with their ideas and interpretations of literature.

This round table discussion is designed to meet many needs in different educational settings and on many academic levels. It is a nonthreatening, social motivational tool which will promote reading and will help students develop an aesthetic appreciation of literature.

Guidelines for Round Table Discussion

1. Each student should be given a reading list to review.

2. The class should be given time to coalesce. Each student should decide on an author and find other students interested in the same author.

3. The students should be allowed to go to the library to find books. The librarian and teacher should have already coordinated the availability of resources, but the students should decide which specific books they will be reading. For example, if a group were reading books by Ernest Hemingway, one person might read *The Sun Also Rises,* one might read *A Farewell to Arms,* and one might read *The Old Man and the Sea.*

4. The teacher should give the class a specific amount of time to read the book.

5. Each student should be given a *vocabulary list* of literary terms pertinent to the processes involved in the round table discussion.

Vocabulary List for
Round Table Discussion

Each student needs to define the following literary terms:

1. Setting

2. Temporal

3. Plot

4. Characterization

5. Conflict
   A. Man vs. Man
   B. Man vs. Himself
   C. Man vs. Society
   D. Man vs. Nature

6. Point-of-View
   A. First Person
   B. Third Person
   C. Omniscient
   D. Limited Omniscient

7. Theme

8. Allusion

9. Irony

10. Inference

11. Comparison

12. Contrast

13. Symbolism

14. Genre

Questionnaire

Name _____
Date _____
Period _____

1. Title: 2. Author:

3. What is the setting of your book?

4. Discuss the basic plot (overview).

5. Describe a character in your book. Give physical description, personality, etc. Use adjectives; give reasons.

6. What is a conflict in your book (man vs. man, man vs. himself, etc.)? Why?

7. What is the point of view (first person, omniscient, etc.)?

8. Discuss a theme from your book.

9. Describe any symbolism used in your book.

10. How is your book similar or dissimilar to the other books read by your group?

Student Critique

Students should use this form to critique each other. This will encourage students to pay attention and motivate them to read a book which has been recommended by a peer.

Name	Author/Title	Setting	Character	Theme	Point of View

6. Each student will also complete a questionnaire about his book.

7. The students will be given time to meet as a group and discuss how *all books* are alike and different.

8. Each group will take part in a round table discussion to inform the class about their author and the books that they have read.

9. As each group makes a presentation, the other students in the class will be listening and completing the critique form. Every student is involved. Speaking, listening, writing, and reading skills are involved in this group discussion.

Book Reviews

Fiction Review

You are to use your own paper to answer the following questions concerning your book. You are to write neatly, spell correctly, and use correct punctuation. Your answers are to be written in complete sentences. You are to write in ink. Skip a line between each answer.

As a journalist, you have been given the assignment of writing a review of the book that you have just read. Answer the following questions and try to be impartial.

1. What is the title of your book?

2. Who is the author of the book?

3. How many pages are in the book?

4. What is the book's main setting? Give the place and the time period.

5. Explain a major change that a main character goes through in the course of the book. Include what causes the change.

6. Explain a truth or insight about life that you have learned by reading this book.

7. Who is your favorite character and what is it that you like about him/her?

8. Explain 3 major conflicts in the book. Give an example of each conflict.

9. Use Weak, Fair, Good, Very Good, and Excellent to answer the following questions.

A. Was the plot exciting?

B. Were the characters interesting?

C. Was the book at the appropriate reading level for you?

10. Do you recommend this book to other readers? Comments, please.

General Essay Questions

1. Discuss two different settings described in the book. Explain how and why these settings are significant to the plot and in the understanding of the book.

2. People in real life are constantly changing and learning. Discuss major changes a character goes through. Is he generous, honest, cruel or kind? What did he learn and how did he change?

3. Write a description of a minor character that will describe what you think of him. What is the relationship between the minor character and the major character? Why is this minor character interesting to you?

4. Define irony and discuss an example of how irony is used in the book.

5. What would you say is the most exciting or dramatic incident in the book? How did the author make it exciting? Show how the author builds up suspense and tension.

6. Is there an especially humorous or frightening character or scene in the book? Describe him or it.

Drama Review

All answers are to be written in complete sentences. Spelling, punctuation and grammar usage are very important. Skip a line between each answer.

1. Give the play's title.

2. Give the author's name.

3. How many acts are in the play?

4. How many characters are in the cast?

5. What is the time period of the play?

6. If producing the play, how many sets are required? *Briefly* describe them.

7. Who is/are the protagonist/s?

8. Who or what is the major antagonist?

9. Imagine you are a famous director. Who would you cast in the roles of the protagonist and antagonist?

10. Explain the major conflict within the play.

11. Define the literary term climax and then identify the scene that marks the climax of the play. Cite the act and scene in which it occurs.

12. State one theme from the play.

13. What character would you most like to portray in the play? Explain why.

14. What scene within the play would you most like to see performed? Give a brief reason why.

15. Did you like the play? What was one strength? What was one weakness?

16. Would you expect this play to be a hit on Broadway? Why or why not?

Symbolic Collage

An artistic production to culminate the round table discussion is a symbolic collage.

Instructions:

1. Poster board divided into four parts will be placed in front of the class. The students can choose any authors that they have studied.

Example:

Twain	Poe
London	Dickens

2. Each student will be given an envelope which contains various materials such as colored construction paper, tissue paper, textured materials, straw, etc.

3. The instructor will ask the student to select something from his envelope that he thinks best represents the author in a specific quadrant.

4. These materials will be glued or stapled in that quadrant of the poster board. The results will vary.

5. Unlimited discussions will be generated about why certain colors, textures, etc., symbolize each author.

6. Each class can display a collage that represents its interpretation, and classes can compare and contrast each other's interpretation of the authors' literature.

Banned Books

Many books are commonly censored from high school and college libraries because of controversial material. Ironically, these are often the books that students relate to and enjoy most. Many classic books are commonly banned from libraries because the language or themes are offensive to certain populations.

One way to get students to read more avidly is to introduce classic literature which commonly appears on banned book lists. The American Library Association publishes a listing of all books which have frequently been banned in the United States. The ALA publication is entitled *Cele-*

brating the Freedom to Read. These banned books are not R-rated; they are classics such as *Of Mice and Men, The Diary of Anne Frank,* the Holy Bible, *The Catcher in the Rye,* and *Romeo and Juliet* (see list). Certain aspects of these books and plays were found to be objectionable to certain populations.

Encouraging students to openly discuss the issues surrounding censorship, and specifically censorship in classic literature, promotes reading.

High schools and colleges can form a Banned Book Club devoted to understanding why books are censored. Members will read controversial books and will analyze why those books were found to be a threat to certain groups of people. Following are some suggestions on how to incorporate a Banned Book Club in school.

1. Librarians and teachers will sponsor the club's activities.

2. Promotional activities for the club can be held through English classes and through daily announcements.

3. Students may pick up an application from the librarian.

4. Regional authors, college instructors, community leaders, and students may present unique analyses and lead discussions about the controversial literature.

5. Teacher/student polls can be taken to discover what the favorite books of the teachers and students are, and to find out if these books appear on Banned Book lists.

6. Bulletin board displays can be made of the data collected in the teacher/student poll. The favorite work or books of different grade levels (freshman, sophomore, etc.) can be displayed. This can be a motivational tool for the students.

7. Debates can be held between students and faculty/parents under the supervision of the sponsors and/or officers of the club. Debate topics can include a certain book, the issue of censorship, moral values in literature, etc.

8. Writers' workshops could be organized in which local artists can display their work and be available for discussion and consultation.

What better way to understand human nature and help young adults reach maturity than to freely discuss controversial themes and issues under educational and parental guidance and supervision.

Commonly Banned Books

Brave New World, Aldous Huxley. Considered a "sex" novel.

The Catcher in the Rye, J. D. Salinger. Vulgarity, occultism, violence and sexual content.

Catch-22, Joseph Heller. Objectionable language.

Clan of the Cave Bear, Jean M. Auel. Sexual content.

The Color Purple, Alice Walker.

Themes about race relations, God, African history, and its sexual content.

The Crucible, Arthur Miller. Often banned because the play contains "sick words from the mouths of demon-possessed people."

Death of a Salesman, Arthur Miller. Profanity.

The Diary of Anne Frank, Anne Frank. Sexually offensive material.

East of Eden, John Steinbeck. Considered "ungodly and obscene" by detractors.

A Farewell to Arms, Ernest Hemingway. Often labeled a "sex" novel.

Flowers for Algernon, Daniel Keyes. Explicit, distasteful love scenes cited.

Flowers in the Attic, V. C. Andrews. Contains "offensive passages concerning incest and sexual intercourse."

Forever, Judy Blume. Said to contain "four-letter words and talk about masturbation, birth control and disobedience to parents."

Grapes of Wrath, John Steinbeck. Inappropriate language and an unfavorable picture of a former minister.

The Holy Bible. Violence.

Huckleberry Finn, Mark Twain (Samuel Clemens). Objectionable language and "racist" content.

Harriet the Spy, Louise Fitzhugh. Lying, spying, and cursing.

I Know Why the Caged Bird

Sings, Maya Angelou. Said to advocate a hatred for the white race.

The Living Bible, William C. Bower. "A perverted commentary on the King James version."

Lord of the Flies, William Golding. It is said to preach that man is not much more than an animal.

The Martian Chronicles, Ray Bradbury. Profanity and the use of God's name in vain.

Nineteen Eighty Four, George Orwell. Pro-communist views and sexual content.

Of Mice and Men, John Steinbeck. Profanity.

One Day in the Life of Ivan Denisovich, Aleksandr Solzhenitsyn. Objectionable language.

One Flew Over the Cuckoo's Nest, Ken Kesey. Violence.

Ordinary People, Judith Guest. Cited as obscene and depressing.

The Pigman, Paul Zindel. Novel concentrates on dishonest characters.

The Red Pony, John Steinbeck. Sexual content.

A Separate Peace, John Knowles. Sexual content and offensive language.

Slaughterhouse-Five, Kurt Vonnegut. Violence, sex, and profanity.

That Was Then, This Is Now, S. E. Hinton. Objections to language, subject, and immorality.

To Kill a Mockingbird, Harper Lee. Cited as harming race

Banned Book Club
Application

Name:

Grade:

1. What are your views on censorship?

2. What is your favorite book? Have you read any interesting books this year?

3. Would you be able to attend meetings after school on Wednesday? Preferred time?

4. Why do you want to be a member of the Banned Book Club?

We are looking for people who are truly interested in understanding censorship. Members must be willing to spend time reading books and articles about the authors.

Student/Teacher Poll

Name:

Please list your four favorite books. List your most favorite first, then second favorite and so on.

1.

2.

3.

4.

I give the Banned Book Club permission to use my selections of favorite books in the announcements throughout the school year.

_____

signature of student/teacher

relations and having inappropriate language.

Ulysses, James Joyce. "Given its long history of censorship, *Ulysses* has rarely been selected for high school libraries. With the new edition, I would anticipate problems"—Judith Krug, Director, Office for Intellectual Freedom, ALA (1986).

Uncle Tom's Cabin, Harriet Beecher Stowe. Use of the word "nigger."

Where the Sidewalk Ends, Shel Silverstein. Said to undermine adult authority.

Friends of the Library

At the beginning of each year librarians and teachers can send out a questionnaire to parents and patrons asking about their interest in involvement with library activities. The interested people should be contacted and a meeting arranged to discuss literary activities and programs for the year. Needs of the library can be assessed and committees should be formed to accommodate these needs. Suggested committees:

1. Phone—to call parents and arrange specific times to work in the library.

2. Finance—to create programs to make money and promote interest in the library's financial needs.

3. Book donations—to encourage the community to contribute books to the library.

4. Honoree donation—to honor or pay homage to an individual.

5. Memorial donation—to memorialize a deceased community leader, educator, student, patron, or friend of the library.

6. Program—to develop programs to encourage censorship debates, guest speakers, author discussions, presentations by publishers, book reviews, film documentaries created by local citizens, or any topic relevant to individual library needs.

Friends of the Library is an endeavor organized for the promotion of library use and, specifically, reading. The more the community is involved, the more students, parents, educators, and citizens of the community will feel like the library belongs to them.

III. Study Skills

Educators seem to agree on the importance of study skills in the educational arena. Study skills are educational habits. These habits begin very early in a child's world. Parents probably influence the student's study skills more than anyone or anything else. The child learns to listen, discriminate and make decisions before he begins formal educational training. He learns to manipulate his world and influence those around him. He realizes that certain tools may be needed to meet his objectives. These tools may be crayons, pencils and paper when he first goes to school. Being equipped with these materials may be one of the first organizational tasks of formal education.

Study skills encompass many sectors, from holding a pencil and paper to discriminating between important and trivial knowledge. Listening, writing, reading, note taking, outlining, and test taking are a few of the skills which assist the student in the classroom. If we as educators have to stop our instruction and say, "We need a class on study skills," we may indeed need to evaluate and change our entire curriculum.

There are no formal study skills programs in most schools. This may be a difficult problem to overcome since so many variables are present. This chapter concentrates on skills which are important for students to emphasize in their daily classroom routine.

Time Profile

Organization can be taught at a very early age. Two-year-olds can separate the forks from the spoons. Six-year-olds can easily fold and sort towels and wash cloths. Children of these early ages are not too young to be taught about the responsibility of organization. When children are taught the importance of being organized and responsible at an early age, they are usually reliable students throughout their education.

One reason students are academically dysfunctional is because they do not organize their time. It might be helpful for students to see how they

Time Profile

Time	Day 1	Day 2
5:30–6:00 A.M.		
6:00–6:30		
6:30–7:00		
7:00–7:30		
7:30–8:00		
8:00–8:30		
8:30–9:00		
9:00–9:30		
9:30–10:00		
10:00–10:30		
10:30–11:00		
11:00–11:30		
11:30–12:00 Noon		
12:00–12:30 P.M.		
12:30–1:00		
1:00–1:30		
1:30–2:00		
2:00–2:30		
2:30–3:00		
3:00–3:30		
3:30–4:00		
4:00–4:30		
4:30–5:00		
5:00–5:30		
5:30–6:00		
6:00–6:30		
6:30–7:00		
7:00–7:30		
7:30–8:00		
8:00–8:30		
8:30–9:00		
9:00–9:30		
9:30–10:00		
10:00–10:30		
10:30–11:00		
11:00–11:30		

How Did You Spend the Past 48 Hours?

Category	Time Spent (T)	Hours T/48	T×60	Minutes ?/2880×100=?%	
Example: Eating	3 hrs	3/48	3×60=180	180/2880	16%
1. Eating	_____	_____	_____	_____	_____
2. Watching T.V.	_____	_____	_____	_____	_____
3. Being out-side	_____	_____	_____	_____	_____
4. Reading	_____	_____	_____	_____	_____
5. Sleeping	_____	_____	_____	_____	_____
6. Playing or listening to music	_____	_____	_____	_____	_____
7. Studying	_____	_____	_____	_____	_____
8. Playing or watching sports	_____	_____	_____	_____	_____
9. Talking on phone	_____	_____	_____	_____	_____
10. Working	_____	_____	_____	_____	_____
11. Socializing	_____	_____	_____	_____	_____
12. Other	_____	_____	_____	_____	_____

Evaluate your time:

1. How did you spend most of your time? _____
   What percent of your time was spent in this activity? _____

2. How did you spend the least amount of time? _____
   Percent? _____

3. How much time did you spend studying? _____%

4. From your analysis, what are four things you can do to utilize your time more effectively?
   A. _____
   B. _____
   C. _____
   D. _____

spend their time and how their lives are constantly governed, either directly or indirectly by elements of time. This can be accomplished by having each student complete a time profile in which he keeps track of how he spends his time for two days.

Students often have problems organizing their time in an acceptable order. They watch television before they do their homework. They talk on the phone knowing that they should be studying for an exam. They have problems with prioritizing time and arranging their activities in the order that is best for their set of circumstances.

Hopefully, the student will get a clear picture of what he can do to better utilize his time. He may need to eliminate certain activities and spend more time on others.

Positive Attitude

A student's ability to achieve in an educational environment depends upon many variables, one of which is having a positive attitude. This attitude can be affected by the teacher's acceptance of and respect for the individual student. A positive attitude is reciprocal. Educators and parents need to work together for the benefit of the student. Most school systems do not have courses on developing and maintaining a good attitude. However, having a good attitude is fundamental to being a good student, a lifetime learner and a happy person in society. Educators need to be aware of the importance of complimenting the student and letting him know he is respected as a person. The student needs to be told on a regular basis that his work and efforts are worthwhile.

Organization and Setting Priorities

It is not the responsibility of the parent or teacher to keep up with a student's assignments. Theoretically, by the time he reaches middle school, the student should be able to budget his time and complete his homework assignments promptly. But, that, in many cases, is not reality!

Many students need to be diverted towards good study and organizational habits. One way a student can get organized is to complete an assignment calendar. He should have the calendar with him throughout the school day to assist in keeping up with current classroom assignments.

Some students have a problem prioritizing their activities. This may be fostered by students who want to become involved in too many activities or by parents who encourage their child to participate in too many extracurricular activities. Problems may arise when these extracurricular activities

Name: _____

SUBJECT	MONDAY	TUESDAY	WEDNESDAY	THURSDAY	FRIDAY	POSITIVE RESPONSE
ENGLISH						
MATH						
SCIENCE						
HISTORY						
OTHER						

interfere with and become more important than academics. In addition to extracurricular activities, more and more students have joined the work force after school. Most students do not work more than five or six hours a day, but that work time eliminates valuable study time.

Another priority in many young adults' lives is their television time. They rush home from school to watch their favorite shows.

Extracurricular activities, work, and television are not the only bad habits that consume a teenager's time. Many teens spend a large amount of time on the phone or just "hanging out."

Good study skills begin with setting the proper priorities. If the student spends too much time on extracurricular, work related, or social activities, his academic life often suffers. Educators and parents need to emphasize that the student's main responsibility and first priority should be academics.

A positive way to call attention to good study habits is by utilizing a dramatization or play, presented by the students' peers. Students are usually bored by the traditional study skills, lectures and materials, which are not self-motivating. Kids will usually listen to other kids. It can be a boost to some students to realize that their buddies are making similar choices and priorities concerning valuable time.

Following is a short example of a dramatization concerning study habits which could be performed in a classroom, for an entire class or student body, to an elementary audience, for parent/teacher organizational meetings, or for any special group.

Central School Study Zone

SETTING: A large room with smaller areas or centers where all students are preoccupied with various activities.

MUSIC: *Twilight Zone* music

As the music plays, the drama begins.

NARRATOR: Welcome to Central School's study zone. We are here to share some important information which may help students become more competent. Study skills are learned skills for the purpose of acquiring knowledge or competence. Study skills involve specific techniques and behaviors which can be objectively described and measured. These skills help students learn more effectively.

Let's take a look at a few study skills or habits and see how they apply to the student's study environment.

Meet Joe and Anna. They have a problem with scheduling time.

Preparedness Quiz

If a teacher has a large percentage of students who come to class unprepared, she might give a daily grade for preparedness by using the following questions.

1. Did you have the correct book with you? (10 points)

2. When the bell rang to begin, were you seated at your desk with book open to correct place, paper prepared to take notes, and pencil ready? (10 points)

3. Did you have all of your homework or assignments prepared to turn in? (20 points)

4. Did you have your body turned in such a way to constantly make eye contact with the teacher as she lectured? (20 points)

5. Did you participate in class discussion or question/answer session? (10 points)

6. Was your educational experience a positive and wonderful one today? (10 points)

7. Was your behavior in class impeccable, extraordinary, and exemplary? (20 points)

Give yourself a grade on how well prepared you were today. Shoot for 100% every day in every class.

JOE: But Anna, I'm going to look over the material tonight before I go to bed. I'll do fine on the test.

ANNA: Joe, Mrs. Smith reminded you Friday that you would have to make at least an 80 on the exam to pass. You haven't spent any time preparing for the test.

JOE: It's okay. I know this material from listening in class. I'll study right before the exam.

NARRATOR: Joe waits until the last minute to study. He usually does okay except for courses which require more concentrative studying. Time could be his enemy because he doesn't consider how important it is to prepare for the exam.

***

NARRATOR: Another problem students have may be the T.V. Listen to this conversation.

BETTY: Do you think we should study now or finish this movie? Alan, I'm tired, so maybe we need to study now before I fall asleep.

ALAN: Okay! *(Turning T.V. off.)* I'll tape this movie and we can watch it later when we have free time.

NARRATOR: Remember to always schedule your studying for the time when you work best. Analyze your patterns of mental energy and fatigue. Some people are morning people and they can get more done at this time. Others are night people and they work better and accomplish more in the evening.

***

NARRATOR: Meet Telephone Eddie!

EDDIE: Yes! Yes! Uh hum . . . I know!! Yeah!! *(Talking on phone.)*

NARRATOR: Eddie does this every night. He calls at least 5 people per night . . . before he studies. He could be a successful student but he uses all of his time on the phone.

***

FRED: *(Wearing baseball hat and glove — throwing ball in the air.)* If we had had 5 more minutes left in the game we could have won by a landslide. We were on a roll.

GINA: Are you going to be able to play in the next game? Are your grades up to par?

JAMIE: I've heard the administration is going to check each player's grades for a "C" average.

FRED: I'm not worried. The teachers will help me! They know I want to play real BAD!

ELIZABETH: But Fred. . . You need to help yourself by studying. What's more important — sports NOW or your FUTURE?

***

Scott and Stacie are studying at a table.

STACIE: I need to write a report but I can't find the correct word in this dictionary.

SCOTT: You need to get a thesaurus or a special dictionary for this assignment.

NARRATOR: Reference books can help you study and can also build your vocabulary. Remember that vocabulary is a large part of all national standardized tests.

***

Bill, Trent, and Cindy are working together.

BILL: We've got a report tomorrow but I say we go to the mall and see who we can see. We'll come back and work on the paper. We'll have plenty of time.

TRENT: Bill, you've said that before.

CINDY: Let's write the paper before we go to the mall.

***

Lights go down on stage.

NARRATOR: *(Spotlight on narrator.)* All of these students have a common bond. They are all students who have better things to do than study. They are preoccupied with extracurricular activities, sports events, T.V., socializing, and other things which students enjoy. Nevertheless, they all know that they have a major responsibility to fulfill academic requirements.

Our cast would like to give you some positive feedback about good study habits.

JOE: Our lives are filled with many responsibilites and we all know that we have to discipline ourselves and put effort into the subject we are studying or we pay the consequence.

ANNA: We would like to share some study tips which could help each person become a more successful student. We would like to emphasize to you that effective study skills are not unreach-

CAST:

able goals. They are habits. A person who consciously strives to achieve good study skills will be able to study smarter, not harder.
Study smarter — not harder!

***

NARRATOR:

Do you ever feel like you are in a twilight zone? Change that! Tune into the Central School study zone to learn how.

ANNA & JOE:

Schedule your study for the time when you work best, not when your energy is at a low ebb.

BETTY & ALAN:

Your study area should be isolated as much as possible from household activity and noise.

EDDIE & ELIZABETH:

Keep reference books close at hand. Dictionaries can aid you in better written and oral presentations.

FRED & GINA:

You will find that studying is easier if you make it more active. Passive study, silent reading and memorization offer too many opportunities for distractions which can be external, such as noise, or internal, such as daydreams.

STACI & SCOTT:

Active study involves the use of several senses. The more senses you involve in your learning, the more long lasting it will be.

BILL & TRENT:

Good notes should be neat, well-organized, concise, clear and as accurate as possible. Be selective in what you write down.

JAMIE & CINDY:

Read material you especially want to remember several times. Then close your book or notebook. Recite to yourself in your own words what you have understood. As you read a paragraph, look for the topic sentence.

NARRATOR:

Improve your vocabulary. As you read, circle new or technical words which are unfamiliar to you. Vocabulary is important in all areas. Vocabulary building will help you on the PSAT and other national examinations.

Notetaking

Notetaking and listening are skills which are required for effective studying. One has to listen to decipher the message. Using interpretive skills to distinguish between the relevant and irrelevant is a critical analysis process which depends upon good listening habits.

The process of notetaking and listening can be effective if you can involve as much *active* learning as possible. The following activity may help with the interpretive and organizational process of collecting relevant information. This process is called mapping. The teacher or a student will read the folllowing paragraph aloud. Everyone should listen.

"The first miniature golf course was atop Lookout Mountain on the border of Georgia and Tennessee. It was on Fairyland Inn which is now known as the Fairland Club on Lookout Mountain. T. N. Garret Carter patented his course under the trade name Tom Thumb Golf."

1. What is the main idea of the paragraph? Place the main idea in the circle.

2. What are some supporting facts? Place those on the lines around the circle.

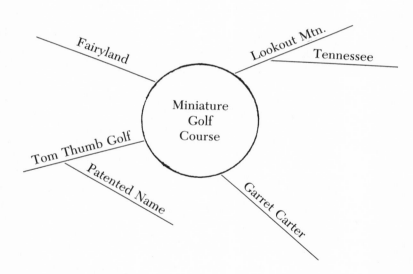

Memory Skills

Developing a good memory is a key component to being a proficient student. Many memory games are available; one that could be used in a classroom by teachers or at home by parents is an old game used frequently at gatherings of young people.

The first player makes a statement (i.e., "Columbus sailed the ocean blue"). The next player must add something to that statement, "Columbus sailed the ocean blue in 1492." The next player adds something new, "Columbus sailed the ocean blue in 1942 on the Santa Maria," and so on. Each student adds something new. The statements can be factual or fiction; it is the listening and remembering that are important.

The first player to incorrectly recall the sequence is "out." The last player to get all of the sequence correct is the winner.

Having a good memory takes practice and discipline. If you can make a game out of improving memory, students will look forward to the competition and improved ability.

If teachers and librarians use this game on a regular basis, it greatly enhances the students' ability to remember sequences of events and promotes an awareness of good listening and memory skills.

Another game is called *Memory Match*. This game can be adapted for all age groups, primary level through college.

The students or players are given a board which can be made in minutes by teachers or parents. (See example) Whatever subject is being studied or tested can be used in the square. The example given shows authors and books. The student will match up the appropriate author with the correct title. The monitor can use "post-it" adhesives with numbers to cover the answers.

The first student begins by calling out two numbers (i.e., 21 and 27). When the monitor removes the "post-it," the student sees the name "Tom Sawyer" under #21 and under #27 he sees "John Steinbeck." Do they go together? No. The next player has an opportunity to choose two numbers. He may choose #20 as the first number. Under #20 he sees *"The Grapes of Wrath."* He should remember that John Steinbeck was under 27. So, that would probably be his next number. Since he successfully paired the author with the correct title or vice versa, he earns 10 points. Each member of the team will continue this process until all numbers have been removed and the correct terms have been successfully paired together.

A student can also play the game by himself.

The game can be used with definitions and words for a vocabulary study. A history student can create a board with dates and events. A time limit could be put on the game.

This activity increases concentration and memory skills, which help increase test scores. The memory match game is an effective way for parents, students, and educators to become more involved with concentration and memory skills.

Study Skills Test

To study well, you need to develop discipline and perseverance. Good study skills are essential to being a competent and effective student. By practicing, you can develop good study habits and improve your grades in school. Take this test and see if you need help. Be honest.

	Usually	Sometimes	Never
1. I study in a quiet environment.	____	____	____
2. I set aside time every day to study.	____	____	____
3. Good grades are a priority with me.	____	____	____
4. I use special books (dictionary, thesaurus, etc.) regularly.	____	____	____
5. I have a special place to keep all my assignments.	____	____	____
6. I budget my time well.	____	____	____
7. I spend more time studying than on the phone or socializing.	____	____	____
8. I have a mature attitude towards school.	____	____	____
9. I take notes in class.	____	____	____
10. I interact with my teachers and my peers.	____	____	____
11. I want to be a success at school and in life.	____	____	____
12. I am making plans for my future.	____	____	____
13. I try to make the best decisions possible.	____	____	____
14. I am reliable with my assignments.	____	____	____
15. I listen to my parents.	____	____	____
16. I am a good listener.	____	____	____
17. I know what's going on in class.	____	____	____
18. I have my books and work organized.	____	____	____
19. I concentrate while the teacher is lecturing.	____	____	____
20. I see the importance of a good education.	____	____	____
21. I participate in group discussions and projects.	____	____	____
22. I try to be an independent library user.	____	____	____
23. I ask questions if I don't understand.	____	____	____
24. I try to evaluate my progress on a regular basis.	____	____	____
25. I feel good about myself, because I am someone special.	____	____	____

Go over the questions and analyze your study habits. Give yourself two (2) points for every "usually"; one (1) point for every "sometimes"; and zero (0) points for every "never."

Great study habits	45–50 points
Good study habits	35–45 points
Pretty good study habits	30–35 points
Okay study habits	25–30 points
Could be better	20–25 points
HELP!	15–20 points
The Pits!	0–10 points

Alice Walker 1	Scarlet Letter 2	Mary Shelley 3	Canterbury Tales 4	Thomas Hardy 5	1984 6
George Orwell 7	Native Son 8	Frankenstein 9	Hamlet 10	Tess 11	Charles Dickens 12
Richard Wright 13	The Great Gatsby 14	Mark Twain 15	Eudora Welty 16	Chaucer 17	A Christmas Carol 18
F. Scott Fitzgerald 19	The Grapes of Wrath 20	Tom Sawyer 21	The Color Purple 22	Shakespeare 23	Profiles in Courage 24
Invisible Man 25	Delta Wedding 26	John Steinbeck 27	Nathaniel Hawthorne 28	Ralph Ellison 29	John F. Kennedy 30

Study Skills Bibliography

The Arco Editorial Board. *High School Equivalency Diploma Tests*. Arco, 1966.

Armstrong, William Howard. *Study Tips*. Barrons's Educational Series, 1983.

Bateman, Barbara D. *The Essentials of Teaching*. Dimensions, 1971.

Bee, Clifford. *Secondary Learning Centers*. Goodyear Publishing, 1980.

Bender, Michael. *Teaching Functional Academics*. University Park Press, 1982.

Berger, James L. *Educators Guide to Free Audio and Video Materials*. 28th ed. Educators Progress Service, 1981.

Bergmann, Sherrel. *Decision-Making Skills for Middle School Students*. National Education Association, 1985.

Bishop, Leslee J. *Staff Development and Instructional Improvement*. Allyn and Bacon, 1976.

Bisschop, Marijke, and Theo Compernolle. *Your Child Can Do It Alone*. Prentice-Hall, 1983.

Blatt, Burton. *In and Out of the University*. University Park Press, 1982.

Boehm, Ann E. *The Parent's Handbook on School Testing*. Teachers College Press, 1982.

Bragstad, Bernice Jensen. *A Guidebook for Teaching Study Skills and Motivation*. Allyn and Bacon, 1982.

Brawner, Julianne Rand. *The Kudzu-Ivy Guide to Southern Colleges*. Kudzu-Ivy, 1982.

Brenton, Myron. *What's Happened to Teacher?* New York: Coward-McCann, 1970.

Canfield, Jack. *100 Ways to Enhance Self-Concept. . .* Prentice-Hall, 1976.

Canoles, Marian L. *The Creative Copycat*. Libraries Unlimited, 1982.

Classroom Management. Educational Testing Service, 1983.

The College Blue Book. 19th ed. Macmillan Publishing, 1983.

DeBruyn, Robert L. *You Can Handle Them All*. Master Teacher, 1984.

Devine, Thomas G. *Teaching Study Skills.* Allyn and Bacon, 1981.
————. *Teaching Study Skills.* Allyn and Bacon, 1982.
————. *Teaching Study Skills.* Allyn and Bacon, 1987.
Duke, Daniel. *Classroom Management.* Random House, 1984.
Ehly, Stewart W., and Stephen C. Larsen. *Peer Tutoring for Individualized Instruction.* Allyn and Bacon, 1980.
Entwistle, Harold. *Child-Centered Education.* London: Metheun, 1970.
Fantini, Mario D., and Gerald Weinstein. *The Disadvantaged.* New York: Harper and Row, 1968.
Flesch, Rudolf Franz. *How to Write, Speak, and Think More Effectively.* Harper, 1960.
Fox, Robert S. *School Climate Improvement.* P.D.K., n.d.
Friederich, Willard J. *Teaching Speech in High Schools.* Macmillan, 1953.
Functions of the Placement Committee in Special Education. National Association of State Directors of Special Education, 1976.
Gagne, Robert Mills. *The Conditions of Learning.* New York: Holt, Rinehart and Winston, 1965.
Gerhard, Muriel. *Effective Teaching Strategies with the Behavioral Outcomes Approach.* West Nyack, NY: Parker Publishing, 1971.
Good, Thomas L., and Jere E. Brophy. *Looking in Classrooms.* 2d ed. Harper, 1978.
Graham, Kenneth G. *Study Skills Handbook.* International Reading Association, n.d.
Gross, Ronald. *The Independent Scholar's Handbook.* Addison-Wesley, 1982.
Hassett, Joseph D., and Arline Weisberg. *Open Education.* Prentice-Hall, 1972.
Heinemann, Robert B., and Marilyn Bernstein. *The Fourth R.* Boston: Beacon Press, 1967.
Hertzberg, Alvin, and Edward F. Stone. *Schools Are for Children . . .* Schocken Books, 1971.
Hopkins, Charles D., and Richard L. Antes. *Classroom Testing.* Peacock Publishers, 1979.
Hyde, Margaret Oldroyd. *My Friend Has Four Parents.* McGraw-Hill, 1981.
Ilg, Frances I., and Louise Bates Ames. *School Readiness.* Harper, 1965.
Johnson, David W. *Circles of Learning.* Association for Supervision and Curriculum Development, 1984.
Johnson, Stuart R., and Rita B. Johnson. *Developing Individualized Instructional Material.* 1st ed. Palo Alto, CA: Westinghouse Learning Press, 1970.
King, Martha L. *Informal Learning.* Bloomington, IN: Phi Delta Kappa Educational Foundation, 1974.
Kourilsky, Marilyn L., and Elizabeth F. Berry. *Classroom Learning Centers.* Educational Resource Association, 1973.
Laslett, Robert. *Effective Classroom Management.* Nicholas, 1984.
Lessinger, Leon M. *Every Kid a Winner.* New York: Simon and Schuster, 1970.
Levine, Samuel. *Vocational and Technical Mathematics in Action.* New York: Hayden Book, 1969.
Likert, Rensis. *The Human Organization: Its Management and Value.* McGraw, 1967.
Lovejoy's Career and Vocational School Guide. New York: Simon and Schuster, 1967.
Lovejoy's College Guide. New York: Simon and Schuster, 1970.
McMullin, Rian, and Bill Casey. *Talk Sense to Yourself.* Rev. ed. Jefferson County Mental Health, 1975.
Meacham, Merle L., and Allen E. Wiesen. *Changing Classroom Behavior.* Scranton: International Textbook, 1969.

Mitchell, James V. *Tests in Print III.* The Buros Institute of Mental Measurements, 1983.

Osipow, Samuel H. *Theories of Career Development.* New York: Appleton-Century-Crofts, 1968.

Peter, Laurence J., and Raymond Hull. *The Peter Principle.* New York: W. Morrow, 1969.

Phillips, E. Lakin, and Daniel N. Wiener. *Discipline, Achievement, and Mental Health.* Prentice, 1961.

Preston, J. B. *Academic Therapy.* AGS, 1979.

Purkey, William Watson. *Self-Concept and School Achievement.* Englewood Cliffs, N.J.: Prentice-Hall, 1970.

Schinke, Steven Paul. *Life Skills Counseling with Adolescents.* University Park Press, 1984.

Sergiovanni, Thomas J. *Handbook for Effective Department Leadership.* Allyn and Bacon, 1977.

Shaughnessy, Mina P. *Errors and Expectations.* Oxford University Press, 1977.

Smith, Judith M., and Donald E. P. Smith. *Child Management.* Research Press, 1976.

Strope, John L., Jr. *School Activities and the Law.* The National Association of Secondary School Principals, 1984.

Terman, Lewis M., and Maud A. Merrill. *Stanford-Binet Intelligence Scale.* 3d rev. Houghton, 1973.

Turner, David R. *High School Equivalency Diploma Tests.* Arco, 1975.

Valleutti, Peter J. *Teaching Interpersonal and Community Living Skills.* University Park Press, 1982.

Wehan, Paul. *Vocational Curriculum for Developmentally Disabled Persons.* University Park Press, 1980.

Westerman, Gayl S. *Spelling and Writing.* Dimensions, 1971.

Wilen, William W. *Questioning Skills for Teachers.* NEA Professional Library, 1987.

Wynne, Edward A. *Looking at Schools.* Lexington Books, 1980.

IV. Research

Research means a careful or diligent search or a critical inquiry. When attempting a research project, it is imperative for students to understand that the base word of research, "search," means to probe or to hunt; and that the prefix, "re," means again and again.

Research should be a building process, and the student should continually be exposed to research techniques. A teacher should not wait until the student's senior year in high school and automatically expect him to produce a 2,000 word term paper never having gone through the process of research before.

Our approach to research is individualistic and may be in contrast with the philosophy being practiced in many schools. However, we feel very strongly that research should not be taught in an isolated manner. Research should be taken a step at a time during the entire school year. Students need as many research experiences as possible. If teachers would follow this rationale throughout middle and high school years, college students would be able to function more independently in the library.

It is with this premise in mind that we approached this section of the book. The student will be completing several research projects before attempting a finished paper. In each research project new skills will be introduced and developed. By the end of the year, the student will have completed several such projects and will be ready to master independent research.

A healthy relationship between the teacher, student, and librarian is important. They should communicate constantly about projects. Working as a team, the teacher and librarian can expose students to a variety of teaching methods, personalities, and ideas. Teachers and librarians need to consciously incorporate flexibility, patience, and respect in their planning and teaching.

Reteaching is an important aspect of research. This can be easily accomplished by tutoring those students who need extra help and reteaching in small groups. Using this reteaching procedure, other students can continue at their own pace.

Research: One Step at a Time

Research	Time	Topic	Requirements	Skills	Project
PROJECT 1	Sept. Oct. 2 days	Famous Person	3 sources 8 note cards 200 words	Bibliography Note Taking	Bibliofile
PROJECT 2	Nov. Dec. 3 days	The 1300s–1600s	5 sources 15 note cards 400 words	Thesis Outline	Time line
PROJECT 3	Jan. Feb. 4 days	The 1700s–1900s	7 sources 20 note cards 700 words	End notes Rough draft	Newspaper
PROJECT 4	Mar. Apr. 5 days	The 1900s–Infinity	9 sources 30 note cards 1000 words	Finished Product	Create

The topics and activities in this chapter are suggestions, which may or may not fit exactly into your curriculum. The building process, however, is the key to successful research.

Project One

Selecting a Topic

The first step in completing research is selecting a topic. Many teachers find it easier to assign a general topic to the student in the initial stage of research. Assigning a general topic, but allowing the student to choose a specific topic within the general one, permits supervised flexibility. When a student knows nothing about appropriate research methods and the teacher allows him to choose any topic from any discipline, the student is often overwhelmed by the vast amount of topics available. Also, the library may not have enough information or resources to support each topic.

A famous person would be an easy topic to begin researching. For an English class, students could find information on famous writers. This allows students to become familiar with writers through research rather than teacher lecture. For science, history, philosophy, or sociology, the student could research a famous person in that area to enhance his knowledge in each specific discipline.

Following is a list of famous person topics from several disciplines:

Literature

Louisa May Alcott
Victor Hugo
Sidney Lanier
Henry James
Stephen Crane
Richard Wright
Mark Twain
Emily Dickinson
Alice Walker
Percy Shelley
Edgar Allan Poe
Langston Hughes
Kate Chopin
J. D. Salinger
Ernest Hemingway

Ralph Ellison
S. E. Hinton
Sylvia Plath
J. R. Tolkien
Stephen King
John Keats
Emily Brontë
Pearl Buck
Richard Bach
John Steinbeck
Thomas Hardy
Emile Zola
Charles Dickens
Lewis Carroll
Robert Frost
James Baldwin
Tennessee Williams

Willa Cather
F. Scott Fitzgerald
Sherwood Anderson

Math/Science

John Napier
Pythagoras
Euclid
Archimedes
Sir Isaac Newton
Karl F. Gauss
Janos Bolyal
George Boole
Kurt Gödel
Charles Babbage
Gregor Mendel
Louis Pasteur
Albert Einstein
Enrico Fermi
Hippocrates
James Watson
Francis Crick
Nicolaus Copernicus
Johannes Kepler
Andreas Vesalius
Ptolemy
Archimedes
Michael Faraday
Joseph Henry
Heinrich Hertz
Robert Boyle
Carl Scheele
Galileo Galilei
Marie Curie
Carolus Linnaeus
Joseph Priestley
Niels Bohr
James Clerk Maxwell
Leonardo da Vinci
Alexander Fleming
Sir Frederick Augustus
   Abel

History

Hirohito
Suharto
Margaret Thatcher
Fidel Castro
John F. Kennedy
Ayatollah Khomeini
Mikhail Gorbachev
Gaddafi
Lucy Stone
Susan Anthony
Elizabeth Stanton
Lucretia Mott
Martin Luther King
George Patton
George Washington
Jim Crow
Carl Stokes
Thurgood Marshall
Andrew Young
Malcolm X
Stonewall Jackson
Winston Churchill
Jean Bart
Ivan V
Sebastoam Pombal
Abraham Lincoln
Queen Victoria
Joan of Arc
Maria Teresa
Mother Teresa
Barbara Jordan
Adolf Hitler
Mohandas Gandhi
Andrew Carnegie
Joseph Stalin

Sociology/Psychology

Max Weber
Herbert Spencer
Emily Baich

Margaret Mead
Talcott Parsons
Auguste Comte
W. E. B. DuBois
Emile Durkheim
Gunnar Myrdal
Franklin Frazier
Charles Johnson
David Hilbert
Jules Henri Poincaré
George Cantor
Robert Merton
Vilfredo Pareto
Talcott Parsons
William G. Sumner
William James
Sigmund Freud
John Dewey
Jean Piaget
Benedict de Spinoza
Jacques-Bénigne Bossuet
Lucretia Mott
Lucy Stone
Susan B. Anthony
Plato
Alvin Toffler
Fulton Sheen
John Naisbett
Jean Cocteau
Theodor Relk
Mortimer Adler
Ivan Petrovich Pavlov
William Masters
Alfred Charles Kinsey

Philosophy/Religion

Immanuel Kant
Plato
Roger Bacon
Aristotle
Anaxagoras
Pythagoras
Anselm (Saint)
Peter Abelard
John Locke
Gabriel Marcel
Bronson Alcott
Karl Marx
Blaise Pas
Theodore Parker
Bertrand Russell
Jean-Paul Sartre
Voltaire
G. W. F. Hegel
John Dewey
Rene Descartes
Albert Camus
Martin Buber
Gottfried Wilhelm Leibniz
Thomas Hobbes
Charles de Montesquieu
Jacques Bossuet
Billy Graham
Mother Teresa
Moses
Hugo Grotius
Giambattista Vico
Benedict de Spinoza

Forming Work Groups

Learning is an interrelated process involving curricula, students, and educators. Students not only learn from teachers and books, but also from each other.

During the initial research project, students should work together in small groups. Each person will participate in individual research and will also work in small groups assisting peers with the new skills introduced. Working in groups builds confidence, especially with complicated processes such as completing a bibliography and taking notes.

Having an alternative to homogeneous grouping allows for basic, average, and high achievers to work together building tutorial skills and self-esteem. Each teacher will have to consider his population and each student's individual needs.

The students should be divided into small groups of three or four persons. The teacher should assign a high-achiever to each group. The students can sign up to work in groups on the following sign-up list. Note that space is provided on the sign-up list to assist in monitoring progress.

The teacher will assign each group a question to research about their person. Each group should try to be as thorough as possible in answering the question and evaluating the factual accuracy of the information that they are researching.

Research Questions

1. Evaluate this person's childhood. Could you detect any traumatic incidents involving his early years?

2. Analyze this famous person's family interrelationships and conclude if his unique family situation had a bearing on his future.

3. Summarize the famous person's educational training.

4. Interpret whether your famous person's nationality influenced his notoriety.

5. Classify your famous person as an introvert or an extrovert, making a judgment about his personality.

6. Determine if your famous person was family oriented by analyzing his marriage or marriages.

7. Appraise his political viewpoints. Did his political involvement affect his success?

8. Evaluate your famous person's life and decide if he could have had any dark secrets in his past.

9. Analyze your famous person's death. Were any abnormalities involved?

10. How did your famous person affect the world?

In order to guarantee success and eliminate unnecessary frustration, the teacher, librarian, and student must work together considering grade level, academic achievement level, and resources available in the library.

Sign Up List
Famous Person

Student's Name	Research Question or Questions	Skills Completed Note Cards	Bibliography
Group 1.			
1. _____	_____	___	___
2. _____	_____	___	___
3. _____	_____	___	___
Group 2.			
1. _____	_____	___	___
2. _____	_____	___	___
3. _____	_____	___	___
Group 3.			
1. _____	_____	___	___
2. _____	_____	___	___
3. _____	_____	___	___
Group 4.			
1. _____	_____	___	___
2. _____	_____	___	___
3. _____	_____	___	___
Group 5.			
1. _____	_____	___	___
2. _____	_____	___	___
3. _____	_____	___	___
Group 6.			
1. _____	_____	___	___
2. _____	_____	___	___
3. _____	_____	___	___
Group 7.			
1. _____	_____	___	___
2. _____	_____	___	___
3. _____	_____	___	___
Group 8.			
1. _____	_____	___	___
2. _____	_____	___	___
3. _____	_____	___	___
Group 9.			
1. _____	_____	___	___
2. _____	_____	___	___
3. _____	_____	___	___

WORKING TOGETHER

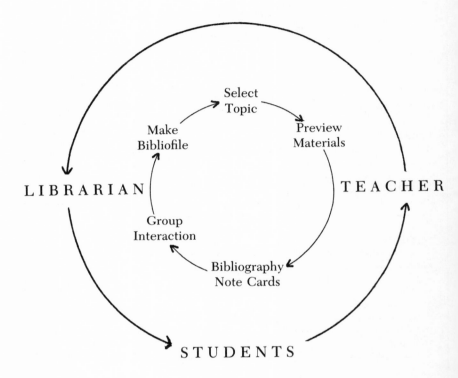

Bibliography Cards

As the student begins research in the library, she will preview relevant information about her famous person determining the credibility of the resources. When she finds a credible source, the student will begin by making a bibliography card.

A bibliography card is a 4″ × 6″ or 3″ × 5″ index card that documents the author of a book or article, the title of the book, the copyright date, where it was published, etc. This information is written down on the card. Bibliographies contain exact information in an exact order.

On a bibliography card, titles of books, encyclopedias, and magazines are underlined. Shorter works, like articles in magazines and encyclopedias, titles of short stories, and musical compositions have quotation marks.

The first source used in the research project should have an "A" placed in the upper right hand corner of the card. A "B" appears on the second card, and a "C" is on the third card. The first line of the information should touch both margins and the remaining lines should be indented.

Students should be encouraged to fill the bibliography cards out exactly. If the student learns to do it correctly in the initial stages of research, it will be to his advantage throughout his educational career.

The following is a list of bibliographic entries that may be used as a guide when creating bibliographies:

Book by one author
Fleet, Ryan. *Running for the Gold*. Rome: Myth Press, 1976.

Book by more than one author
Runningbear, Joe, and Loni Arrow. *An Indian Dance*. University of New Mexico Press, 1988.

Essay within a collection of pieces by different authors
Gold, Henry. "Search for Wealth." In *Treasure Hunt*. Travis Seek and Maggie Find, eds. New York: Sunken Harbor Books, 1984.

Edition of a work of literature
Love, Jason. *Lonely Heart*. Joann Coeur, ed. Sidney: Hope Classics, 1923.

Article in an encyclopedia or other reference work
Pin, Gail. "Porcupines." *Encyclopedia of American Animals*. 1986 ed.

Article from a monthly magazine
Ladder, Bobby. "New Shades of Blue." *Painting Today*. April 1980, p. 19.

Article from a newspaper (no author given)
"President Visits Local High School." *Hometown Gazette*. 6 May 1990, p. 1.

Review of a film, book, or play
Rise, Sonny. Revision of *Looking for Morning*, by Sheila Glasses. *Search*. 14 July 1987, p. 42.

Interview
Reid, Leslie. Librarian. Personal interview. *World of Bibliographies*. 30 September 1984.

Radio or television program
"Hillbilly Hoedown." *Evening Dance Party*. DYR. 23 Jan. 1979.

Pamphlet
U.S. Cong. House. Report on National Debt, by I.O. Ewe. Washington, D.C.: GPO, 1979.

Research Project One:
Famous Person

Name: _____
Class: _____

Progress Report

A. Skills

                                                Date Due:

   1. Note Cards   _____
   2. Bibliography cards   _____

B. Put a check beside all of the library resources that you have used for this project. You MUST include the resources listed in capital letters.

       1. ENCYCLOPEDIA   _____
       2. DICTIONARY   _____
       3. CARD CATALOG   _____
       4. Readers' Guide   _____
       5. Text on Microfiche   _____
       6. Humanities Index   _____
       7. SIRS   _____
       8. CD ROM   _____
       9. Databases   _____
     10. Online Search   _____
     11. Dialog   _____

C. Keep a time line of your progress during this research assignment. Budget your time properly.

<—————————————————————————————————>
beginning date of research   completed assignment

Note Cards

Each note card should have at the center top, a topic heading of what is discussed on that note card. Notes should be legible and may be abbreviated. Each note card should have a reference page number to show the source and page the information was taken from.

The student should now have a clear understanding of the initial steps of research. He has researched a famous person and should know how to complete bibliography and note cards.

The teacher and librarian should monitor the student's progress and be available for consultation. It is imperative, however, that the student work as independently as possible. Good library habits will produce independent lifetime library users.

The teacher may wish to use a progress report (see page 82) to assist the student in monitoring his own progress, resources, and time.

Bibliofile Documentary

After the student collects his information, he will return to the classroom and work together in groups to present an oral presentation answering the assigned questions about the famous person. Since the questions appear in chronological order according to the famous person's life, the presentations should also appear in the same order. Each presentation can be videotaped. The videotape collection will become the bibliofile documentary.

The bibliofile documentaries can be stored in the library or media center. Videotapes should be available to teachers who should be encouraged to interchange bibliofiles with each other for use in the classroom. Students should also be encouraged to view or check out all bibliofile documentaries across the curriculum.

Project Two

After the students have been exposed to the research process and have learned to complete bibliography and note cards, they are ready for the next steps in the research process.

On page 84 is a list of interdisciplinary topics of the time period from the 1300s to the 1600s and a sign up sheet for students. The teacher should pass the list around the room, letting each student choose a topic of interest. The sign up sheet is designed to assist the teacher in record keeping.

Research project two will encompass the bibliography and note card skills introduced in the initial research project. In addition to these skills,

Sign Up Sheet
1300s to 1600s

	Student's Name	Topic	Thesis	Skills Outline
1.	_____	Christopher Columbus	____	_____
2.	_____	Hundred Year's War	____	_____
3.	_____	Geoffrey Chaucer	____	_____
4.	_____	Black Death	____	_____
5.	_____	Aztecs	____	_____
6.	_____	The Bastille	____	_____
7.	_____	Alchemy	____	_____
8.	_____	Globe Theater	____	_____
9.	_____	Joan of Arc	____	_____
10.	_____	Hubert Van Eyck	____	_____
11.	_____	Byzantine Empire	____	_____
12.	_____	Leonardo da Vinci	____	_____
13.	_____	Johannes Gutenberg	____	_____
14.	_____	King Arthur/fact or legend	____	_____
15.	_____	Gunpower Inventions	____	_____
16.	_____	Nostradamus	____	_____
17.	_____	Council of Trent	____	_____
18.	_____	William Shakespeare	____	_____
19.	_____	Sir Walter Raleigh	____	_____
20.	_____	John Calvin	____	_____
21.	_____	Spanish Armada	____	_____
22.	_____	Magna Carta	____	_____
23.	_____	James I—King James Bible	____	_____
24.	_____	Ann Boleyn	____	_____
25.	_____	War of the Roses	____	_____

two new concepts will be introduced: writing a thesis statement and writing a formal outline.

Thesis Statements

A thesis statement is a complete sentence summarizing the main idea of a paper. It clearly shows the point-of-view of the writer. The thesis should be proven throughout the paper with facts, ideas, and expert opinions. The thesis statement should be in statement form, not in question form, and it must be detailed and exact.

Most students will change the thesis statement, often several times, as they get more and more involved with the research process. But it is best to write a thesis statement early in the research process because it helps the student stay focused on elements of the topic that he is researching.

Examples:

Good thesis statement: specific

The traumas that Charles Dickens endured during childhood helped the writer become acutely aware of injustices to children and to prisoners, both of which are depicted clearly in two of his novels, *Great Expectations* and *Oliver Twist*.

Bad thesis statement: general

Charles Dickens was a nineteenth century British writer who wrote many fascinating books.

Good thesis statement: specific

Although Henry Ford has been considered an American hero, he was an egotistical business tycoon.

Bad thesis statement: general

Henry Ford made a lot of money off of the automobile industry.

Good thesis statement: specific

Elvis Presley's unique style contributed to the development of rock and roll music.

Bad thesis statement: in question form

Thousands of people have sighted Elvis in twenty-two cities across the U.S.; they all want to know, is Elvis alive?

Outlines

An outline is information that lists the order of the points to be discussed in a research paper. An outline uses Roman numerals first (I, II, III), then capital letters (A, B, C), next Arabic numbers (1, 2, 3), then small letters (a, b, c) to show the order, relationship, and importance of ideas.

Two types of outlines are generally used: a sentence outline and a topic outline. A sentence outline states each topic and subtopic in a complete sentence. A topic outline states each heading with only words and phrases.

Some common problems that students have with outlining are problems with alignment, capitalization, and numbering/lettering. In aligning an outline, the periods of the Roman numerals should be exactly aligned. This takes some planning, especially when typing the paper. In outlining, the first word of each topic is always capitalized; after that, only the proper nouns should be capitalized.

Another problem that commonly arises with outlining is with numbering and lettering. The "golden rule" of outlining is that you cannot have a one without a two, and you cannot have an A without a B. If you have a major topic I, you must have a major topic II. (Refer to example.)

Example.

William Shakespeare

I. Childhood
   A. Parents
      1. Mother
      2. Father
         a. Uneducated
         b. Glovemaker
   B. Education
      1. Studied languages
      2. Grammar school
II. Marriage
   A. Age
   B. Ann Hathaway
   C. Children
      1. Twins
         a. Judith
         b. Hammet
      2. Susanna
III. Moved to London
   A. Globe Theater
   B. Performer
IV. Famous works
   A. Romeo and Juliet
   B. Hamlet
   C. Macbeth

After the new skills have been introduced, the student should go to the library and begin researching his topic for the 1300–1600 time period. The student should make bibliography and note cards, write a thesis statement and write an outline.

Research Project Two: 1300s to 1600s

Name: _____

Class: _____

Progress Report

A. Skills

Date Due:

1. Note Cards _____
2. Bibliography cards _____
3. Thesis Statement _____
4. Title Page _____
5. Outline _____

B. Put a check beside all of the library resources that you have used for this project. You MUST include the resources listed in capital letters.

1. Encyclopedia _____
2. Card catalog _____
3. Dictionary _____
4. READERS' GUIDE _____
5. TEXT ON MICROFICHE _____
6. HUMANITIES INDEX _____
7. SIRS _____
8. CD-ROM _____
9. Databases _____
10. Online Search _____
11. Dialog _____

C. Keep a time line of your progress during this research assignment. Budget your time properly.

$\longleftarrow$ _____ $\longrightarrow$

beginning date of research   completed assignment

Time Lines

A culminating classroom activity for research project two could be to make a time line in which the entire class can be involved. Butcher paper or art paper can be taped along the wall of the classroom. The teacher can outline the time line with major dates (see below), and the student can individually place his research topic on the appropriate place on the line.

1300   1616   1699

Shakespeare's
Death

The student could also give an oral report on his research findings, while the rest of the class takes notes on the presentation. Grades may be taken on the bibliography, note cards, oral presentation, thesis statement, outline, written paper, independent library use, or class participation. The oral presentation of the research findings could be videotaped and added to the bibliofile documentaries. All grades are optional and depend upon the teacher's time allotment and priorities. Many skills are involved in this type of activity: writing, listening, speaking, and analysis of events.

After completing research project two, the student will spend time in the classroom completing his regular class assignments for that discipline. It is important for the students' time to be integrated between classroom and library activities. This new approach to independent library use, as compared to the standard once-a-year approach, should prevent research burnout.

Project Three

Research project three is an interdisciplinary project that will encompass the time period of the 1700s through the 1800s. This research project will be especially challenging because it involves actually writing the rough draft of the research paper. Processing the notes into complete sentences and paragraphs can be a frustrating experience even for a polished writer, but especially for a novice.

Too much emphasis cannot be placed on teacher and librarian patience and flexibility. The teacher and librarian are the initiators and motivators in the research aspect of library use, and their attitudes toward progress and acceptable work often determine whether the student will put forth his best effort. This is not to imply that students are not self-motivated, because they are; but, if the student feels totally overwhelmed by the often

Sign Up Sheet
1700s–1800s

Student's Name	Topic	Skills Rough Draft	Endnotes
1. _____	Queen Victoria	_____	_____
2. _____	England & Common Market	_____	_____
3. _____	Ghenci	_____	_____
4. _____	Clive of India	_____	_____
5. _____	Victorian Morals	_____	_____
6. _____	Charles Dickens	_____	_____
7. _____	Civil War	_____	_____
8. _____	Lord Nelson	_____	_____
9. _____	Mark Twain	_____	_____
10. _____	Herman Melville	_____	_____
11. _____	Nathaniel Hawthorne	_____	_____
12. _____	Percy Shelley	_____	_____
13. _____	John Keats	_____	_____
14. _____	Industrial Revolution	_____	_____
15. _____	Abraham Lincoln	_____	_____
16. _____	Harriet Tubman	_____	_____
17. _____	Underground Railroad	_____	_____
18. _____	U. S. Grant	_____	_____
19. _____	Battle of Chattanooga	_____	_____
20. _____	Specific Civil War Battle	_____	_____
21. _____	Eli Whitney	_____	_____
22. _____	Tuberculosis	_____	_____
23. _____	Child Labor Laws	_____	_____
24. _____	Victorian Furniture	_____	_____
25. _____	Napoleon	_____	_____

cumbersome processes involved in writing the research paper, he can become frustrated. Research should be a challenge, not an automatic defeat.

Rough Draft

To begin writing the rough draft, the student should have completed the outline and note cards. He should spread the note cards out somewhere with plenty of room. There should be no order to the note cards to begin with.

The student should find all of the note cards that pertain to I (the first major topic in her outline). Put these cards in a stack and set them aside. Then, find all of the note cards that go with II. Put these in a separate stack. Follow this process until all of the major topics in the outline have a corresponding stack of note cards.

The stack which correlates to the main topic I should be arranged in order according to the subtopics (A, B, C) in the outline. Arrange each major topic and subtopics in the order that the paper will be written. The student should then write the rough draft by changing the notes into his own words and documenting or endnoting the specific information.

The thesis statement may need to be revised. Some teachers prefer to wait until the paper has been written to complete the thesis statement, which is in the introductory paragraph.

The student needs to ensure that each paragraph relates to the thesis statement and that each section is linked to the previous one through a transitional statement. Each research paper should include a concluding paragraph which sums up the most important aspects of the paper. This paragraph should prove or disprove the thesis statement.

Endnotes

Endnotes are notes found at the end of a paper to cite or show the source of material. The following information should be documented with an endnote to show where the student got that specific information:

1. Direct quote
2. Opinion
3. Information or facts not generally known
4. Idea that is not your own

Endnotes are found on a separate endnote page that is found near the end of the research paper. Each endnote should have a reference page number which shows exactly where the student got that specific information. Endnotes are indented like paragraphs. The first name of the author should come first and the last name comes last. Students often get this

Student Critique of Rough Draft

A = Acceptable Work
NP = Needs Improvement
U = Unacceptable

Name of student who wrote paper _____

I. Topic of paper _____
II. Organization of paper _____
III. Thesis statement _____
IV. Bibliographic cards_____
V. Required references _____
VI. Notecards
   A. Proper form _____
   B. Topic heading per card _____
   C. Page number on each card_____
   D. Quality of information_____
   E. Recurring grammar problem _____
VII. Writing of paper
   A. Abbreviations spelled out _____
   B. Title page in correct form _____
   C. Direct quotes in quotation marks _____
   D. Footnotes in correct form _____
   E. Organization of paper_____

Comments: _____
Do you think the teacher needs to talk with the student about plagiarism before he/she turns in the final product?

_____

Signature of students critiquing paper.

_____   _____

_____   _____

Research Project Three:
1700s–1800s

Name: _____

Class: _____

Progress Report

A. Skills

                                          Date Due:
    1. Note Cards   _____
    2. Bibliography Cards   _____
    3. Thesis Statement   _____
    4. Title Page   _____
    5. Outline   _____
    6. Endnotes and Rough
       Draft   _____

B. Put a check mark beside each library resource that you used for this project. You MUST use each of the resources listed in capital letters.

     1. Encyclopedia   _____
     2. Dictionary   _____
     3. Card Catalog   _____
     4. Readers' Guide   _____
     5. Text on Microfiche   _____
     6. Humanities Index   _____
     7. SIRS   _____
     8. CD-ROM   _____
     9. Databases   _____
    10. ONLINE SEARCH   _____
    11. DIALOG   _____

C. Keep a time line of your progress during this research assignment. Budget your time properly.

$\longleftarrow\!\!\!\longrightarrow$

beginning date of research   completed assignment

procedure confused with the bibliographic form, which is almost the opposite. Endnotes should appear within the paper after the last word that needs to be documented. They are numbered consecutively throughout the paper. The actual endnote number should be elevated about one-half of a line above the regular line.

Example:
[1]Lewis Driver, *Parallel Parking Made Easy* (New York: Automobile Press, 1990), pp. 14–32.
[2]Will I. Crash, "The Perfect Intersection," *Safe Driving*, September 1991, p. 15.
[3]Driver, p. 14.

Student Critique Sheet

A student critique sheet (p. 91) can be used in a small group for critiquing the rough draft. We suggest that one high-achieving student be deliberately placed in each group of three to five students. This will insure that each research paper has been looked over or critiqued by a competent student. This process will save the teacher time in grading the papers, will promote peer tutoring and cooperative learning, and will help develop leadership.

Newspaper

A culminating activity that may be used in correlation with the 1700s–1800s research project could be the production of a classroom newspaper. Each student could contribute articles or information about his research topic. The class as a whole will have to work to produce a unique documentary of world history. This activity will incorporate speaking, listening, writing, and reading plus journalism skills and cooperative learning across the curriculum.

Project Four

The finished product of a research paper is the refined, edited product of the rough draft. The finished product should always be typed or written in blue or black ink on unlined paper. It should be as professional as possible for the grade and academic level. The student will be utilizing and reinforcing all of the research skills concentrated on throughout three other research projects completed this year: taking notes, making a bibliography, writing a thesis statement and outline, entering endnotes, writing and editing a rough draft, and finally typing a finished product of the research paper.

Project four encompasses the 1900s and beyond. This is a limitless, unique era in history that could easily be researched. This project will be an independent research assignment in which the student is allotted a certain amount of time and works independently in the library monitoring his own progress. The student will be responsible for completing the finished research paper utilizing the skills that he has mastered. A suggested topic list and sign up sheet follow.

1900 and Beyond Topics

1920–1930

Margaret Mitchell
Prohibition (Repeal)
Hitler
New York World's Fair
Great Depression
Black Monday
J. D. Rockefeller
Gandhi's Civil Disobedience
Planet Pluto Discovered
Joseph Stalin
Spanish Civil War
Split Uranium Atom
F. Scott Fitzgerald
Flappers
"Roaring Twenties"
Al Capone
Tennessee Valley Authority
Franklin D. Roosevelt
J. Edgar Hoover — FBI
Abdication of King Edward VIII
19th Amendment — Women's Suffrage

1960

Vietnam War
Robert Kennedy
Lyndon B. Johnson
Saigon
Tet Offensive

Peace Movement
Jimi Hendrix
Watergate
The Beatles
Woodstock
Space Age
Nikita Khrushchev
Bay of Pigs
Fidel Castro
Computers
Flower Children
Haight-Ashbury
Marilyn Monroe
Neil Armstrong
1967 Arab-Israeli War
Civil Rights Movement
Charles Drew
Little Rock, Arkansas
Malcolm X
Martin Luther King, Jr.
"I Have a Dream"
NAACP
"Black Revolution"
Jim Crow Laws
Civil Rights Act 1960
Montgomery, Alabama, 1964–1968
"We Shall Overcome"
Julian Bond
Andrew Young
Brown vs. Board of Education

Sign Up Sheet
1900 and Beyond

Student's Name	Topic	Skills Completed Finished Product
1. _____	_____	_____
2. _____	_____	_____
3. _____	_____	_____
4. _____	_____	_____
5. _____	_____	_____
6. _____	_____	_____
7. _____	_____	_____
8. _____	_____	_____
9. _____	_____	_____
10. _____	_____	_____
11. _____	_____	_____
12. _____	_____	_____
13. _____	_____	_____
14. _____	_____	_____
15. _____	_____	_____
16. _____	_____	_____
17. _____	_____	_____
18. _____	_____	_____
19. _____	_____	_____
20. _____	_____	_____
21. _____	_____	_____
22. _____	_____	_____
23. _____	_____	_____
24. _____	_____	_____
25. _____	_____	_____

"Sit in"
Roy Parlso
Resurrection City
Medgar Wiley Evers
13th and 15th Amendments to the
    Constitution
Equal Employment Opportunity
    Commission (EEOC)

The Future

Floating Cities: Macro Engineer-
    ing
Global Equity: The Developing
    World
Weather Modification

Travel Through Black Holes
Cybernetics
Cloning
Body-mind Biofeedback
Right to Die Movement
Importance of Robotics
Intelligence Pill
Data Deluge
Nuclear Waste
Space Colonization
Extra-Planetary Resources
UFOs
Changing Values
Biotechnology
Alternate Sources of Energy
ESP: Potential of Human Mind

For the final research project the student should be encouraged to create a unique interpretation relating to the information that he has found. Ideas for this project are unlimited. Each student's talents can be utilized however he chooses.

Some suggested ideas are:

Dramatic representation
Art work
Band production
Music presentation
Sculpture
Science project
Newspaper
Battle representation
Computer games/charts
Carpentry skills

Oral reading
Original poetry
Video presentation
Slide presentation
Comic books
Interviews
Time line
Crossword puzzle
Fashion show

Bibliography

Arizona English Bulletin: Back-to-the-Basics in English Teaching, v. 18 — #2. Urbana, IL: National Council of Teachers of English, c1976.

Barzun, Jacques Martin. *The Modern Research*, rev. ed. New York: Harcourt, Brace & World, c1970.

Baugh, L. Sue, Maridell Fryer, and David Thomas. *Handbook for Business Writing*. Lincolnwood, IL: National Textbook Company Business Books, c1986.

Bell, Arthur H., and Roger Wyse. *The One-Minute Business Writer*. Homewood, IL: Dow Jones-Irwin, c1987.

The Best of the Best of Eric, v. 3. Urbana, IL: ERIC Clearinghouse on Educational Management, c1982.

Carter, Candy. *Structuring for Success in the English Classroom.* Urbana, IL: National Council of Teachers of English, c1982.

Common Sense and Testing in English. Urbana, IL: National Council of Teachers of English, c1975.

Drazan, Joseph Gerald. *An Annotated Bibliography of ERIC Bibliographies, 1966–1980.* Westport, CO: Greenwood, c1982.

Dyer, Jean Royer. *Understanding and Evaluating Educational Research.* Reading, MA: Addison-Wesley, c1979.

Evans, Bergen, and Cornelia Evans. *A Dictionary of Contemporary American Usage.* New York, NY: Random House, c1957.

Grammar and Style Guide. Chicago, IL: World Book, c1983.

Graves, Donald H. *A Researcher Learns to Write.* Exeter, c1984.

Hillocks, George. *Research on Written Composition.* National Conference on Research in English, c1986.

Holtz, Herman R. *The Business Writing Problem Solver.* Homewood, IL: Dow Jones-Irwin, c1987.

Kaiser, Artur. *Questioning Techniques.* Claremont, CA: Hunter House, c1979.

Lewis, Norman. *The New Roget's Thesaurus of the English Language in Dictionary Form.* Rev., updated 1978 ed. New York, NY: Putnam, c1978.

Mamchak, P. Susan, and Steven Mamchak. *Encyclopedia of School Letters.* Englewood Cliffs, NJ: Parker Publishing, c1979.

Measures for Research and Evaluation in the English Language Arts. ERIC Clearinghouse on Reading and Communications Skills, National Institute of Education, c1975.

Milosh, Joseph E. *Teaching the History of the English Language in the Secondary Classroom.* Urbana, IL: National Council of Teachers of English, c1972.

Mitzel, Harold E., ed. *Encyclopedia of Educational Research.* 5th ed. New York, NY: Macmillan, c1982.

Mohr, Marian M. *Working Together.* Urbana, IL: National Council of Teachers of English, c1987.

Physicians' Desk Reference. 39th ed. Oradell, NJ: Medical Economics, c1985.

The Reader's Digest Great Encyclopedia Dictionary. Pleasantville, NY: Reader's Digest Association, c1971.

Research on Composing. Urbana, IL: National Council of Teachers of English, c1978.

Research Within Reach: Oral Written Communication. Research and Development Interpretation Service, n.d.

Research Within Reach: Science Education. Research and Development Interpretation Service, n.d.

Roget's II: The New Thesaurus. Boston, MA: Houghton Mifflin, c1980.

Taintor, Sarah Augusta, and Date M. Monro. *The Secretary's Handbook.* New York, NY: Macmillan, c1969.

Urdang, Laurence. *The New York Times Everyday Reader's Dictionary of Misunderstood, Misused, Mispronounced Words.* Quadrangle Books, c1972.

Webster's New World Thesaurus. World Publishing, c1971.

V. Critical Thinking

The mind is constantly challenged with mysteries, options, problems, dates, secrets, and unpredictable circumstances, some of which have easy solutions or answers while others are serendipitous. The human mind has the potential to enhance all aspects of our world and beyond. However, we are not born with the innate ability to transfer information from the concrete to the abstract or to think critically. These skills need to be developed.

Since every aspect of society requires that a person be able to think critically and to solve problems, educators are realizing that more emphasis needs to be placed on critical thinking skills. Critical thinkers are creative contributors to society.

Schools deliberately need to provide opportunities in the classrooms and libraries to foster the development of critical thinking. Students need to be shown how to think critically and creatively.

Accomplishing this may be harder than it would seem because teachers and librarians are often mandated by school systems to cover a certain amount of material in a limited time period. As a result, educators seem to separate curriculum from critical thinking, when the two should be interwoven into everyday classroom instruction.

In this chapter ideas and methods are presented which show educators how critical thinking can be incorporated into any lesson or classroom environment.

Instructional Dramatization

Critical thinking enables one to understand more accurately and truthfully what was, what is, and what can be. One can look at the present, past, and future with an analytical mind when searching for the truth. Critical thinkers should assimilate, investigate, analyze, evaluate, and make predictions about situations which challenge them to confront the unknown. This process is called inductive analysis and procreates critical thinking skills.

Teachers and librarians can work together to present these inductive analysis strategies by using an instructional dramatization. This technique is not dissimilar to role playing, which requires that a person assume a certain identity. In this approach the teacher and librarian will show — not tell — the student the importance of a specific concept: in this case the concept will be developing a critical thinking process. Humor and flexibility are deliberately promoted throughout this dramatization.

When students can relate to a variety of teaching methods or ways to learn, they become more observant and learn to think more critically. Teacher lecture requires little thought on the student's part; but when the student observes an instructional dramatization, especially one that is well-planned and has a specific objective, he is given concrete opportunities to think critically.

SETTING: The students are seated in one section of the library. As usual, they are all waiting quietly and patiently for another lecture on the Dewey Decimal System. They are surprised and aghast to overhear the following conversation as the teacher and librarian talk a little too loudly about a personal problem.

TEACHER: But, it's no big deal.

LIBRARIAN: Wait just a minute. Do you have any information about it?

TEACHER: What for?

LIBRARIAN: I mean, have you checked around with other professionals and investigated the possibilities?

TEACHER: What do you mean investigated? I'm not a private detective.

LIBRARIAN: Well, don't you think it's more important for you to know as much as you can possibly know about it?

TEACHER: What's there to know?

LIBRARIAN: It could be a complicated procedure. It could be dangerous, I'd think.

TEACHER: How? I've heard they just stick a hose in and suck it out. Like a vacuum cleaner.

LIBRARIAN: But that's just what you've heard.

TEACHER: How hard could vacuuming be?

LIBRARIAN: Well, that's what you need to find out. Exactly what the procedure entails. You need to analyze all the facts, and make a better educated decision.

TEACHER: I don't care what they have to do. Just get rid of this cottage cheese. Electrolux it!

LIBRARIAN: (Looking worried) Any procedure can get complicated. This is no exception.

TEACHER: I just want to do it and get it over with.

LIBRARIAN: Listen, let me get you some articles from the most current journals. You read them, study them, evaluate the procedures and risks. Then make a decision.

TEACHER: I don't need all that. I just want my originals.

LIBRARIAN: But when you're making important decisions you need to make the best one you possibly can.

TEACHER: I have made the decision: bring on the giant suction machine.

LIBRARIAN: Come on, Martha! You're an educated person!

TEACHER: What does education have to do with a case of super amorphous white carbohydrates.

LIBRARIAN: Don't rush into this! What if they damage the nerves or something? What if your extremities quit working? You can't predict what might happen because you don't know anything about it.

TEACHER: So what!

LIBRARIAN: I'm serious, Martha. Think critically about this.

TEACHER: Okay, okay! I get the picture. I'll find out more. I'll call around.

Inductive Analysis

After the educators complete the instructional dramatization, they should *first* ask the students, "What was the problem being discussed?" The students must go through a process of inductive analysis in order to determine the problem. They should have deduced that the teacher was considering liposuction.

Hopefully, the students enjoyed this dramatization and will be able to explain the five strategies of inductive analysis which are assimilation, investigation, analysis, evaluation and prediction.

The following questions could be used to help clarify and enhance the understanding of the inductive analysis process.

1. When the teacher began complaining about her problem, what did the librarian suggest that she do? (Gather or collect information — to assimilate.) Why was this suggestion important? (You first have to collect information.)

2. What was the next thing that the librarian told her friend to do? (Investigate.) How do you investigate? Discuss as a group. (Interview, read, make phone calls, use all possible sources.)

3. After the teacher investigates the information what does she need to do with this information? (Analyze it.) Discuss. (Examine credibility, scrutinize any minute facts.)

4. The teacher should have analyzed the problem. (Compare and contrast.) Should she stop here? (No.) What should be the next step? (Evaluate the data and come to some conclusion.)

INDUCTIVE ANALYSIS

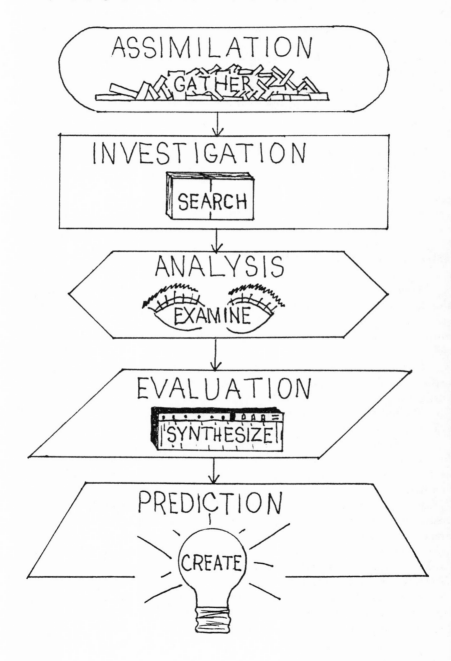

5. A conclusion has been made. How can this conclusion be relevant to the teacher's problem? (Predict outcome by making an informative, educated forecast about the liposuction surgery.)

All students are encouraged to participate in the discussion. The teacher and librarian should strive to show the student how this thinking process should not only be used in an educational environment, but also be incorporated and nurtured in everyday life. Everyone should be aware of good thinking skills. By learning to use the inductive analysis thinking process, the student will learn to be a better thinker.

Inductive Analysis Process

Step 1 Assimilation—data accumulation
    A. libraries
    B. discussions with authorities
    C. telephone
    D. all possible sources
Step 2 Investigation—clarify knowledge
    A. how?
    B. when?
    C. where?
    D. why? why not? why why?
Step 3 Analysis—small integrals of whole
    A. examine
    B. compare/contrast
    C. dissect
Step 4 Evaluation—come to a conclusion
Step 5 Prediction
    A. prognosticate
    B. make an educated and scientific forecast
    C. best educated guess

The mystery of time was chosen as a topic to introduce with critical thinking because it has no limits or boundaries. Time has no beginning or ending—only interpretations. Therefore, the teacher and librarian have an abundance of options when studying time. All subjects across the curriculum can promote critical thinking through the study of time by utilizing the process of inductive analysis. To explore the entity of time provides students with opportunities to go beyond rote memorization or the basic curriculum courses. Exploring the concept of time can only encourage students to think critically and learn to evaluate abstract concepts on the highest levels. Past, present, and future time are presented to help students learn to think critically and creatively.

Past Time

A mysterious topic dealing with past time is Stonehenge. The inductive analysis thinking process can be used with Stonehenge to demonstrate how critical thinking skills can be fostered with any topic.

The puzzle of Stonehenge has been analyzed for centuries. Although the structure is over 5000 years old, controversy still surrounds the mystique of this ancient stone configuration.

Many theories exist concerning the purpose, meaning, uses, and construction of Stonehenge. Some are:

1. It was erected as an astronomical observatory in prehistoric time.
2. Early British kings used it as burial grounds.
3. The Romans built it as a temple to worship the sky god, Coelus.
4. The Danes erected it as a court royal.
5. The Druids made it to house Pagan rites.
6. It was used as a calendar, clock, or time piece.
7. Prehistoric tribes used it as a ceremonial hall and court of justice.
8. The Wizard Merlin arranged for the devil to wish rocks from Ireland at night, hence Stonehenge.
9. Celtic priests used it to salute fire, air, earth, and sea.
10. Pre-Roman priests used it as a pagan castle of power.
11. Astronomer Norman Lorkyer assumes that it was used in relation to the sun.
12. Dr. Stuart Piggott thinks that it has a Greek legendry.
13. It was used as a place for human sacrifice, therefore the name Slaughter Stone.
14. The devil threw a large stone at a friar and struck him on the heel, creating the "Heel Stone."
15. Rituals saluted earth's source of light and warmth in it.
16. It was used as a place for sun worship.
17. It has an Aegean ancestry.

Students love to work with theories. They enjoy proving and disproving information through detective work.

The compilation of theories about Stonehenge is a good place to utilize the inductive analysis thinking process. Individual students or small groups of students can choose a Stonehenge theory to prove or disprove. They need to follow all of the inductive analysis steps using divergent inquiry and the research methods presented in Chapter Four. They should arrive at a conclusion in order to predict the mystery of Stonehenge. The student may want to investigate other theories or, perhaps, create his own.

Present Time

Not unlike Stonehenge, which is a mystery of past time, the crop circles of the Wessex Triangle are enigmas of present time. These unusual circle formations occur frequently, over 400 times during one summer, creating unusual circular patterns, which range from simple circles to more complex bull's-eyes, chains, and beads with connected bars and external arcs. Pinwheel-like circles are apparently blasted and formed from bent, yet unbroken, crops. These mysterious circles are located in close proximity to Stonehenge, and are as baffling today as Stonehenge.

Theories of Crop Circles

Students should choose a crop circle theory and use the inductive analysis thinking process to do further research.

1. Extraterrestrial visitors
2. Extraterrestrial intelligence
3. Testing of Star Wars weapons technology
4. Tornado-like atmospheric conditions
5. Hoaxing
6. Hedgehogs
7. Hippies
8. Fairies dancing through corn
9. Mowing devils who come in the night and cut the crops in rings
10. Atmospheric vortex
11. Whirlwinds
12. Black rodlike things or thongs that jump up and down above the crop
13. Similar to snowflakes
14. Helicopters
15. Circles of the woes of nature's spirit

Using this research information, students should be given time to work in groups to collaborate and build a case for their theory.

Each theory will be presented in debate form.

Comparable theories need to be paired together to debate; this insures a more equitable analysis of the theories. For example: "Fairies dancing through corn" may be paired against "mowing devils who come in the night." "Tornado-like atmospheric conditions" could be linked with the "Star Wars testing" theory.

The following suggested analysis of debate emphasizes critical thinking skills. Teachers may prefer to use their own formats.

Analysis of Debate

	Worst				Best
1. Relevant Information	1	2	3	4	5
2. Reliable Sources	1	2	3	4	5
3. Factual Information	1	2	3	4	5

	Worst				Best
4. Strength of Argument	1	2	3	4	5
5. Inconsistencies	1	2	3	4	5
6. Eye contact-Gestures-Voice Projection-Theatrical Elements	1	2	3	4	5

Comments:

_____

_____

_____

_____

_____

_____

Future Time

Albert Einstein predicted in 1905 that time can be stretched, that it can be affected by the motion of the observer. Scientists have theoretically proven that if you can move faster than the speed of light, your time will move backward.

Just as Jules Verne predicted the use of submarines in his *2000 Leagues Under the Sea*, H. G. Wells' saga of time travel, *The Time Machine*, may have prophesied the revelation of the fourth dimension. Is time travel possible? Can time be reversed? Can we erase mistakes, change history? Can we tunnel forward through space into a future time?

It is very important for students to realize that theories concerning time travel and time, in general, are extremely complex and difficult to comprehend. No indisputable answers, conclusions, or predictions exist — only theories. It could be fun and competitive to go to the library and find out as much as possible about the different theories of time travel.

1. Time can be reversed
2. Quantum mechanics
3. Illusion of neutral kaons
4. Black holes — massive star collapses
5. White holes and black holes run backward in time
6. Anthropic principle
7. Density is infinite
8. Black Power Hypothesis
9. Expansion of universe
10. Creationism
11. Big crunch
12. Special relativity
13. Big Bang Theory
14. Entropy
15. Unified field
16. Grand unified
17. Collapse of universe
18. Fifth dimension
19. Kaluza-Klein
20. Prigogine
21. White dwarf
22. Thermodynamics
23. Neutron star
24. Space warps

Remember, as always, it is imperative to be considerate of students' ideas, regardless of how abstract or absurd they may seem.

Students can use the following questions to assist in collecting data concerning a future time travel. A student may present his theory and its plausibility, discuss similarities and differences in theories, and, hopefully, enjoy the newness of unique and mind-boggling ideas.

1. What is the key word or phrase concerning your theory that you might use in a database search?

2. Define or give background information about your theory.

3. What evidence have you found to determine if your theory is possible?

4. Who are the famous scientists or philosophers who agree with or contribute to your theory?

5. Explain the controversial aspects of your theory.

Poetry Analysis

Teaching a student to think inductively is extremely difficult to do; yet every aspect of one's ability to function in society requires that a person be able to figure out things himself. Answers are not always obvious, but a person should be able to gather facts and solve problems. Certain teaching strategies can help develop better thinking skills. One of these strategies is inductive thinking.

Inductive thinking means figuring out answers to questions by using logic. Students must learn to interpret data, make conclusions, and apply the information. By using this method a student can develop new ways of applying previously learned information.

Inductive thinking can easily be incorporated into most group activities. The teacher can introduce poetry terms by first having the student to define the poetry terms and then discuss the definitions.

allusion	assonance
onomatopoeia	iambic pentameter
metaphor	imagery
simile	jargon
free verse	nostalgia
fable	consonance
personification	dialect
alliteration	symbol
soliloquy	rhythm
denotation	meter
connotation	

After the student defines, discusses, and studies the poetry terms, the class should be divided into groups of four or five students. Each student will be given a group of poetry excerpts. She will discuss the excerpts of poetry with all of the members in her group, and will try to come to a conclusion, using inductive thinking, about which literary term is best represented by the sample of poetry. The teacher could use excerpts from any poem to use with this inductive thinking poetry analysis.

Examples

Poetry Terms with Inductive Thinking

The dark ocean reached into her hot hold.
Answer: Alliteration—*h*ot and *h*old
or
Personification

but the water rose high and cold
Answer: Assonance—rose and cold

Steam from the boilers spewed forth her final sigh
Answer: Personification

Clung to the propellers like dew.
Answer: Simile

"As the cat climbed over
the top of
the jam closet
first the right"—William C. Williams
Answer: Free verse

A fl*oo*r t*oo* c*oo*l for corn
Answer: Assonance

murmur, splash
Answer: Onomatopeia

Tell them youth and glee
Run a course as well as the sea.
Answer: Rhyme or Couplet

Splendor falls on castle halls
Answer: Internal rhyme

clang, bark
Answer: Onomatopoeia

"And the silken, sad uncertain rustling of each purple
curtain . . ."—Edgar A. Poe
Answer: Alliteration

Students must use references and inductive thinking along with the
poetry and information given in order to deduce the correct answers. They
must be able to categorize and interpret new and used data. The teacher
can discuss why and how different groups came up with certain answers.
Explaining the thinking process builds good thinking skills and makes
students aware of the processes involved in using logic.

The teacher serves more as an observer and moderator and should
elicit answers by using appropriate questions. The teacher should also
monitor progress and frustration levels.

Imagery

Critical thinking requires that a person be able to imagine. Imagery is
creating pictures in the mind, awakening and stimulating all senses. The
more senses touched, the more creative the person can be.

Teachers and librarians often fail to nurture and encourage sensory
learning. Sensory learning nourishes critical and creative thinking.
Educators should consciously try to incorporate these types of activities in
their curriculum. Activities which include sensory learning help to increase
retention.

Imaginations can be developed. Therefore, activities are presented in
this chapter which will foster inquisitive and sensory thinking. Perhaps if
educators would utilize a basic type of imagery activity to begin the
development of the imagination, it will be easier for the student to progress
to a higher level of creative and critical thinking.

In closed imagery a student is given a specific detail to visualize. Open
imagery means that *all* sensory options are open to the student's imagination. What he visualizes will depend upon his experiences and background.
Educators need to be aware of the limitations of a student's past. Every student comes into a classroom with unique ideas and personalities, and these
activities provide the perfect place to encourage a student to expound upon
and demonstrate individuality. Educators should utilize these activities in
the ways most suitable to their educational environment.

Closed

Imagine you are there!!!
1. Chanting Druids in a circle with faces turned skyward.
2. Wet grass sticking to Roman type sandals and naked hairy toes.
3. Human sacrifices taking their last breaths lying on a slaughter stone.

4. The Wizard Merlin laughing deliriously wearing a silken robe.
5. Greek soldiers with dirty hands, sparsely attired, digging trenches and carrying stones.
6. Freshly dug dirt being thrown out of a hole.
7. Burial grounds surrounded by circles of stones; ghosts peering back into your eyes.
8. Sun rising above a tree line on a perfectly clear day.
9. A 35-foot-wide time piece sitting in the middle of a football field.

Open

1. Druids in a circle
2. Wet grass
3. Human sacrifices
4. A wizard
5. Greek soldiers

6. Freshly dug dirt
7. Burial grounds
8. Sunrise
9. A time piece

Word Patterns

Another critical thinking activity that can be incorporated into the curriculum which involves all senses and levels of thinking is word patterns. Each student will be given a list of words. This list deals specifically with time; however, a teacher could create his own list from any unit of study.

rituals	solar day	past
heel stone	spectrum	cosmology
Druids	Vikings	round
child labor	Renaissance	boundary
confession	solstice	UFO
apothecary	Darwin	stars
Inquisitions	white holes	clock
Romans	nebulas	light year
Stonehenge	orbit	God
time piece	system	future
pyramids	moon	alien
King Tut	Rabbit Tracks	Isaac Newton
Geronimo	heavens	Polaris
explorers	atom	pendulum
mysteries	circle	Milky Way
Fountain of Youth	galaxies	circles
ice age	present	altar stone
trains	cosmic	circles

midsummer morning	sun	carbon clock
horseshoe	$E = mc^2$	tree ring
earth rampart	white dwarf	prism
moon	Bermuda Triangle	Greek swords
boulder	symmetry	medieval
sun rise	disc	evaluation
conclave	Earth	time travel
geometric	crop circles	black holes
goddesses	spectrum	earthwork
Julian calendar	infinity	atomic clock
carbon	air	zones
hour glass	universe	clouds
gills	time reversals	acceleration
tides	mortise	wavelength
river time	slaughter stone	gamma ray
Nordic	Merlin	cosmological
Victorian	Pope	time
speculation	Protestants	time travel
fantasies	gold rush	imaginary time
worm holes	cowboys	spin
excavation	Indians	dimensions
future	pony express	Star Wars
vacuum	Chaucer	grays
calendar	Roman daggers	gravity
light	simple calendar	big bang
place	hexagon	flat
big crunch	Saxon origin	wave
theory	sun dial	observatory
quantum	Cossacks	death
Omni	hibernation	Anthropic Principle

One way to utilize this list is to have the students categorize words that go together. The students could share with each other their rationale behind choosing groups of words. A student who is not a critical thinker can learn from hearing the verbalized rationale of a person who thinks critically.

Also, students could compare each other's choices of words. This promotes collaborative learning. Example:

White holes	Black Hole	Time Piece
Nebulas	Clock	Observatory
Solar day	Sun Dial	Calendar

Word Linking

Students could also participate in word linking. To begin this game students should be seated in a circle. One student should be chosen to begin the game, and he will choose any word or phrase from the word list. The student seated directly to his right will choose another word from the list that links back to the first word. The second person must give a rationale explaining how the two words or phrases are linked. If she cannot, she is out of the game. The way to determine if a person is out of the game is to take a consensus of the group by a show of hands. The "out" person will have to get a dictionary, encyclopedia, or thesaurus and define both words which she could not link. The person or persons who are left in the circle at the end of the allotted time will be the winners.

Another way to foster creative thinking with vocabulary is the link diagram. Students should write the word that shows the relationship between the three words in the interconnecting space. It is a fun way to help students with logic, vocabulary, analytical thinking, and analogies. Examples:

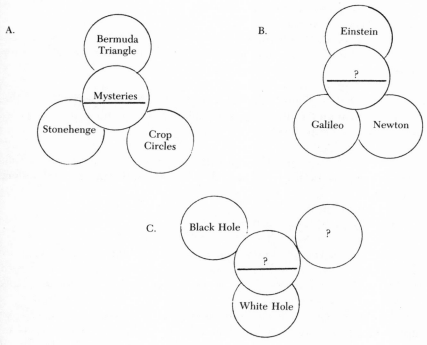

Quotations

Quotations are used in every form of media. An appropriate quote can strengthen practically any argument or presentation. Interpreting and analyzing quotations require critical thinking skills. Many quotation books, including *Bartlett's Familiar Quotations,* are available in school libraries.

Research the following famous quotations about time. Write a paragraph or interpretive paper about the quote and find out who wrote it. Students could also create their own quotations.

1. "It is the wisest who grieves most at loss of time."
   (Dante)
2. "For everything there is a season, and a time for every purpose under the heaven: a time to be born and a time to die..."
   (Ecclesiastes)

3. "So our virtues lie in the interpretation of the time..."
    (Coriolanus)
4. "O for an engine to keep back all the clocks!"
    (Ben Jonson)
5. "You may delay, but time will not."
    (Benjamin Franklin)
6. "Time is Man's Angel."
    (J. C. F. Von Schillen)
7. "Somewhere behind Space and Time is wetter water, slimier slime."
    (Rupert Brooke)
8. "What is Time? — the shadow on the dial, — the striking of the clock, — the running of the sand, — day and night, — summer and winter, — months, years, centuries?"
    (Longfellow)
9. "It is not so much the hours that tell, as the way we use them. Life must be measured rather by Depth than by length: By thought and action, rather the *Time*..."
    (Aveburu)
10. "Though infinite can never meet."
    (Andrew Marvell)

There are several good reference books for quotations; however, they cannot be classified as indexes. Some credible quotation books deal with specific subjects or authors: *The Home Book of Quotations* or *The Home Book of Shakespeare Quotations.*

Quotation books may be arranged in different ways: chronologically or alphabetically by author, or by subject. Bartlett's *Familiar Quotations* is arranged chronologically by author, and Hoyt's *New Encyclopedia of Practical Quotations* and Stevenson's *Home Book of Quotations* are arranged by subject.

Creative Writing

Quotations

Another creative thinking endeavor involves having each student choose one of the following quotes concerning time from the most often read book, the Bible, which was written over 2,000 years ago and deals with the past, present, and future. The student should somehow relate the quote to his own life through writing a personal narrative. For example, a student might choose "A time to mourn and a time to dance," and he could write about the death of a beloved person or animal and the happy times that they shared. The possibilities are limitless.

Each student may read his personal narrative to the class if he wishes. Sharing personal feelings can be a moving experience for many students. Emphasis should be placed on students treating each other with respect and being accepting of others' tender moments. Of course, not all personal narratives will be tear-jerkers, but the teacher should prepare students ahead of time by emphasizing respect for each other.

To every thing there is a season, and a time to every
    purpose under the heaven.
A time to be born, and a time to die;
A time to plant, and a time to pluck up that which is
    planted;
A time to kill, and a time to heal;
A time to break down, and a time to build up;
A time to weep, and a time to laugh;
A time to mourn and a time to dance;
A time to cast away stones, and a time to gather
    stones together;
A time to embrace, and a time to refrain from
    embracing;
A time to get, and a time to lose
A time to keep, and a time to cast away;
A time to rend, and a time to sew;
A time to keep silence, and a time to speak;
A time to love, and a time to hate;
A time for war, and a time for peace.

Ecclesiastes 3:1–8

What If???

"What if" creative writing is a fun way to encourage students to use humor, realism, detail, and imagination in writing. Having students read their stories to the class is a nice way for students, especially the less popular, but very creative ones, to receive recognition.

What if nothing is real unless it is observed?

What if you could go through a time warp back into the past and see your parents as they were as teenagers?

What if you could make an appointment for yesterday and keep it?

What if you could travel to the past and warn Julius Caesar about Brutus' plan to murder him.

What if space has no time, and you could survive for over a billion years?

What if E. T. phoned home? What would his message be?

What if entrophy worked in reverse?

What if you could travel into your worst enemy's mind?

What if time stopped, the world stopped turning, but people still moved and were stuck in the same day forever?

What if there was a secret warp or passage that would take you anywhere you wanted to go?

What if men did not have egos?

What if you could relive one moment in your life? What would it be and why?

What if you died and could haunt one person? Who would it be?

What if Elvis had really died?

What if you could change something about yourself? What would it be? Why?

What if you discovered the lost city of Atlantis where ancient people still roamed, and the doors behind you shut and you were stuck there?

What if you could bring someone from a past time like Abraham Lincoln or John F. Kennedy to the present time? Who would you bring? What would you ask him? What would you tell him?

What if you were a painter and everything you painted became real?

What if you were handcuffed forever to a person you hate?

What if the ozone hole got so big it sucked the earth into space?

What if you were like a VCR and you could rewind, stop, pause, and fastforward your life?

Comparison/Contrast Composition

The purpose of comparison/contrast items is to test the students' understanding of the relationship between two aspects of a subject. If you are comparing past and present mysteries, you should discuss the characteristics of both. Listing the ways the two happenings are alike and different will insure that you discuss the same features about both.

Comparison/contrast compositions are usually arranged in one of the following ways: block style or point-by-point style. In using the block style, all arguments or points about one item are blocked together. For example, the writer would completely discuss all aspects of Stonehenge, then discuss all aspects of crop circles.

On the other hand, point-by-point style involves moving back and forth from one item to another, showing how both items are alike or different for each point of comparison before moving on to a second point.

Try to follow these steps when writing a comparison/contrast essay: You should define or identify both items. If terms or items cannot be easily defined, give examples and details to describe them. Decide on points of comparison. Ask yourself how they are alike and how they are different.

Decide before you write whether you will write a point-by-point or a block comparison in your answer or essay.

Choose one of the following and write a comparison/contrast essay:

1) Compare and contrast Stonehenge and crop circles.
2) Compare and contrast crop circles and time travel.
3) Compare and contrast Stonehenge and time travel.

Research and Roleplay

Poets and philosophers have always been obsessed with the passing of and interpretations of time. It would be interesting to see what students can find out about the following characters or professions by researching and then presenting a role play about their findings.

Time

1. A medieval monk observes time through the eyes of nature.
2. A mother observes time as a fleeting face of youth.
3. An astronomer observes time through celestial movement.
4. A minister observes time from Genesis to Revelation.
5. A truck driver observes time through schedules, logs, destinations.
6. An athlete observes time through conquering obstacles.
7. A baby observes time through tactile pleasures.
8. A banker observes time through deposits and foreclosures.
9. A teacher observes time through tears at graduation.
10. A poet observes time through the symbolism of the words.
11. A student observes time . . . impatiently.

Analogies

Analogies involve upper level thinking skills and are found on most standardized tests. An analogy is a likeness in one or more ways between things otherwise unlike. Example:

Bermuda is to Triangle as Milky is to _____.
a. universe   c. Way
b. Earth   d. clock
The answer is *c.* — Way.

Problems:

1. A moon is to a planet as an electron is to _____.
a. a particle   c. a molecule
b. antimatter   d. a nucleus

2. Gravity is to star as heat is to _____.
a. cold   c. South Pole
b. oven   d. space

3. Big bang is to astronomy as relativity is to _____.

a. $E = mc^2$ c. $v = ma$
b. physics   d. biology

    4. A circle is to a cylinder as a square is to _____.

a. geometry   c. a disc
b. Milky Way   d. a cube

    5. Poor is to Steinbeck as _____ is to Fitzgerald.

a. rich   c. party
b. middle class   d. symbolism

    6. Stars are to galaxy as planets are to _____.

a. time   c. rows
b. fourth dimension   d. solar system

    7. Isaac Newton is to Albert Einstein as Moses is to _____.

a. Aristotle   c. God
b. Jesus Christ   d. eternal life

    8. Infinity is to boundary as blackness is to _____.

a. light   c. shadow
b. integers   d. physics

    9. Oxygen is to gas as calcium is to _____.

a. vitamin   c. metal
b. element   d. liquid

    10. Atom is to element as molecule is to _____.

a. compound   c. reactant
b. product   d. precipitate

Answers:

1. D	6. D
2. B	7. B
3. B	8. A
4. D	9. C
5. A	10. A

Bibliography

Ashley, Rosalind Minor. *Activities for Motivating and Teaching Bright Children.* Englewood Cliffs, NJ: Parker, c1973.

Activities to Promote Critical Thinking: Classroom Practices in Teaching English. Urbana, IL: National Council of Teachers of English, c1986.

Applebee, Arthur N. *Writing in the Secondary School: English and the Content Areas.* Urbana, IL: National Council of Teachers of English, c1981.

Basic Writing: Essays for Teachers, Researchers, and Administrators. Urbana, IL: National Council of Teachers of English, c1970.

Bechtel, Judith. *Improving Writing and Learning.* Newton, MA: Allyn and Bacon, c1985.

Berthoff, Ann E. *The Making of Meaning.* Portsmouth, NH: Boynton/Cook, c1981.

Beyer, Barry K. *Practical Strategies for the Teaching of Thinking.* Newton, MA: Allyn and Bacon, c1987.

Calkins, Lucy McCormick. *The Art of Teaching Writing.* Portsmouth, NH: Heinemann, c1986.

Canoles, Marian L. *The Creative Copycat.* Littleton, CO: Libraries Unlimited, c1982.

Chance, Paul. *Thinking in the Classroom.* New York: Teacher's College Press, c1986.

Christenbury, Leila. *Question: A Path to Critical Thinking.* ERIC, c1983.

Courses of Change in Writing. Boynton/Cook, c1984.

Daniels, Paul R. *Teaching the Gifted/Learning Disabled Child.* Rockville, MD: Aspen, c1983.

Duke, Charles R. *Creative Dramatics and English Teaching.* Urbana, IL: National Council of Teachers of English, c1974.

Eight Approaches to Teaching Composition. Urbana, IL: National Council of Teachers of English, c1980.

Emig, Janet. *The Composing Processes of Twelfth Graders.* Urbana, IL: National Council of Teachers of English, c1971.

————. *The Web of Meaning.* Portsmouth, NH: Boynton/Cook, c1983.

Flesch, Rudolf Franz. *How to Write, Speak, and Think More Effectively.* New York: Harper, c1960.

Flower, Linda. *Problem-Solving Strategies for Writing.* New York: Harcourt, c1985.

Frank, Marjorie. *If You're Trying to Teach Kids How to Write, You've Gotta Have This Book!* Nashville, TN: Incentive Publications, c1979.

Frost, Joan. *Art, Books and Children.* Special Literature Press, c1984.

Gallagher, James John. *Teaching the Gifted Child.* 2d ed. Newton, MA: Allyn & Bacon, c1975.

Geuder, Patricia A., ed. *They Really Taught Us How to Write.* Urbana, IL: National Council of Teachers of English, c1974.

Glennon, Vincent J., ed. *The Mathematical Education of Exceptional Children and Youth.* Reston, VA: National Council of Teachers of Mathematics, c1981.

Graves, Donald H. *Writing: Teachers and Children at Work.* Portsmouth, NH: Heinemann, c1987.

Gross, Beatrice, and Ronald Gross, eds. *The Great School Debate.* New York: Simon & Schuster, c1985.

Harrison, Elizabeth. *Self-Expression Through Art.* Peoria, Bennett, c1960.

Hawkins, Thom. *Group Inquiry Techniques for Teaching Writing.* ERIC, c1976.

Hayakawa, Samuel Ichiye. *Language in Thought and Action.* New York: Harcourt, c1964.

Hillocks, George. *Research on Written Composition.* National Conference on Research in English, c1986.

Holt, John Caldwell. *How Children Learn.* New York: Pitman, c1967.

Hopkins, Lee Bennett, and Annette Frank Shapiro. *Creative Activities for the Gifted Child.* Fearon, c1969.

Johannessen, Larry R., Elizabeth A. Kahn, and Carolyn Calhoun Walter. *Designing and Sequencing Prewriting Activities.* Urbana, IL: National Council of Teachers of English, c1982.

Jolly, Brad. *Videotaping Local History.* American Association for State and Local History, c1982.

Jones, John Charles. *Learning.* New York: Harcourt, Brace & World, c1967.

Kane, Thomas S., and Leonard J. Peters, eds. *Writing Prose: Techniques and Purposes*. 4th ed. New York: Oxford University Press, c1976.

Kottmeyer, William. *Decoding and Meaning*. New York: McGraw, c1974.

Langer, Judith A., and Arthur N. Applebee. *How Writing Shapes Thinking*. Urbana, IL: National Council of Teachers of English, c1987.

Learning-Disabled/Gifted Children. University Park Press, c1983.

Liem, Tik L. *Invitations to Science Inquiry*. Lexington, MA: Ginn Custom Publishing, c1981.

Lyons, Robert, ed. *Autobiography: A Reader for Writers*. New York: Oxford University Press, c1977.

Maker, C. June. *Curriculum Development for the Gifted*. Rockville, MD: Aspen, c1982.

_____. *Teaching Models in Education of the Gifted*. Rockville, MD: Aspen, c1982.

Mayber, John S., Nancy B. Lester, and Gordon M. Pradl. *Learning to Write/Writing to Learn*. Portsmouth, NH: Boynton/Crook, c1983.

Myers, Miles. *A Procedure for Writing Assessment and Holistic Scoring*. Urbana, IL: National Council of Teachers of English, c1980.

National Council of Teachers of English. *English for the Academically Talented Student in the Secondary School*. Washington, DC: National Education, c1969.

Neeld, Elizabeth Cowan. *Writing Brief*. Sidney, OH: Scott, c1986.

Papert, Seymour. *Mindstorms*. New York: Basic Books, 1980.

Patterson, Jo. *Why Doesn't an Igloo Melt Inside?* Memphis City School System.

Polette, Nancy. *Exploring Books with Gifted Children*. Littleton, CO: Libraries Unlimited, c1980.

Ponsot, Marie. *Beat Not the Poor Desk*. Portsmouth, NH: Boynton/Cook, c1982.

Raths, Louis E., et al. *Teaching for Thinking*. Westerville, OH: Merrill, c1967.

Reclaiming the Imagination. Portsmouth, NH: Boynton/Cook, c1983.

Roots in the Sawdust. Urbana, IL: National Council of Teachers of English, c1985.

Rubin, Donald L., and William Dodd. *Talking into Writing*. ERIC, c1987.

Sanders, Norris M. *Classroom Questions: What Kinds?* New York: Harper & Row, c1966.

Sigel, Irving E., and Frank H. Hooper, eds. *Logical Thinking in Children*. New York: Holt, c1968.

Stanford, Gene, and Marie Smith. *A Guidebook for Teaching Creative Writing*. Newton, MA: Allyn and Bacon, c1977.

Stephens, John Mortimer. *The Psychology of Classroom Learning*. New York: Holt, Rinehart and Winston, c1965.

Stillman, Peter. *Writing Your Way*. Portsmouth, NH: Boynton/Cook, c1984.

Teaching Writing in All Disciplines. San Francisco, CA: Jossey-Bass, c1982.

Thinking Through Language. Urbana, IL: National Council of Teachers of English, c1985.

Travers, Robert Morris William. *Essentials of Learning*. New York: Macmillan, c1972.

Valett, Robert E. *Effective Teaching*. Fearon Pubs., c1970.

White, Edward M. *Teaching and Assessing Writing*. San Francisco, CA: Jossey-Bass, c1988.

Whitmore, Joanne Rand. *Giftedness, Conflict and the Underachievement*. Newton, MA: Allyn and Bacon, c1980.

Willen, William W. *Questioning Skills for Teachers.* Washington, DC: NEA Professional Library, c1987.

Writing Talk. Portsmouth, NH: Boynton/Cook, c1983.

Zemelman, Steven, and Harvey Daniels. *A Community of Writers.* Portsmouth, NH: Heinemann, c1988.

Selected Bibliography

Arbuckle, Dugald Sinclair. *Counseling: Philosophy, Theory, and Practice.* 2d ed. Boston, MA: Allyn and Bacon, c1970.

Arnold, Joan Hagan, and Penelope Buschman Gemma. *A Child Dies.* Rockville, MD: Aspen, c1983.

Beck, Carlton E. *Education for Relevance—Schools and Social Change.* New York: Houghton, c1968.

Bedley, Gene A. *How Do You Recognize a Good School When You Walk Into One.* Bedley, c1980.

Beery, Keith E. *Models for Mainstreaming.* Denville, NJ: Dimensions, c1972.

Beggs, David W., ed. *Team Teaching.* Indiana University, c1964.

Behavior Resource Guide. Educational Sciences Inc., c1973.

Benjamin, Robert. *Making Schools Work.* New York: Contiuum, c1981.

Biehler, Robert F. *Psychology Applied to Teaching.* Boston, MA: Houghton Mifflin, c1982.

Bishop, Lloyd K. *Individualizing Educational Systems, the Elementary and Secondary School.* New York: Harper & Row, c1971.

Blackham, Garth J., and Adolph Siberman. *Modification of Child and Adolescent Behavior.* 2nd ed. Belmont, CA: Wadsworth, c1975.

Blitz, Barbara. *The Open Classroom: Making It Work.* Boston, MA: Allyn and Bacon, c1973.

Boehm, Ann E. *The Parents' Handbook on School Testing.* New York: Teachers College Press, c1982.

Brawner, Julianne Rand, et al. *The Kudzu-Ivy Guide to Southern Colleges.* Kudzu-Ivy, c1982.

Bredemeier, Mary E., and Harry C. Bredemeier. *Social Forces in Education.* Sherman Oaks, CA: Alfred, c1978.

Broudy, Harry S. *The Real World of the Public Schools.* San Diego, CA: Harcourt Brace Jovanovich, c1972.

Brown, Duane, et al. *Consultation.* Newton, MA: Allyn & Bacon, c1979.

Buford, Thomas O. *Toward a Philosophy of Education.* New York: Holt, Rinehart and Winston, c1969.

Buscaglia, Leo F. *Love.* Thorofare, NJ: Slack, n.d.

Cawelti, Gordon. *Vitalizing the High School.* Association for Supervision and Curriculum Development, c1974.

Chase, Larry. *The Other Side of the Report Card.* Goodyear, c1975.

Chinn, Philip C., et al. *Two-Way Talking with Parents of Special Children*. St. Louis, MO: Mosby, c1978.

Cohen, Judith H. *Handbook of Resource Room Teaching*. Rockville, MD: Aspen, c1982.

The College Bluebook. 19th ed. New York: Macmillan, c1983.

Conger, John Janeway. *Adolescence and Youth*. New York: Harper, c1973.

Cook, David R. *Guidance for Education in Revolution*. Boston, MA: Allyn and Bacon, c1971.

Cook, Myra B. *The Come-Alive Classroom*. West Nyack, NY: Parker, c1967.

Current Trends in School Law. National Organization on Legal Problems of Education, c1975.

Daughtery, Lynn B. *Why Me? Help for Victims of Child Abuse (Even If They Are Adults Now)*. Mother Courage Press, c1984.

Dinkmeyer, Don C. *Child Development*. Englewood Cliffs, NJ: Prentice-Hall, c1965.

Douglass, Harl Roy. *High School Curriculum*. Ronald, c1956.

Durnin, Richard G. *American Education*. Detroit, MI: Gale Research, c1982.

Ebeling, Nancy B., and Deborah A. Hill, eds. *Child Abuse*. Action, MA: Publishing Sciences Group, c1975.

Education-for-Health. Detroit, MI: Gale Research, c1983.

Fairchild, Thomas M. *Managing the Hyperactive Child in the Classroom*. Learning Concepts, c1975.

Filley, Alan C. *Interpersonal Conflict Resolution*. Sidney, OH: Scott, c1975.

Furtwengler, Willis J. *Improving School Discipline*. Newton, MA: Allyn & Bacon, c1982.

Gardner, John William. *Self-Renewal*. New York: Harper, c1964.

Gardner, William I. *Learning and Behavior Characteristics of Exceptional Children and Youth*. Newton, MA: Allyn & Bacon, c1977.

Gatti, Richard D., and Daniel J. Gatti. *Encyclopedic Dictionary of School Law*. Englewood Cliffs, NJ: Parker, c1975.

Gee, E. Gordon, and David J. Sperry. *Education Law and the Public Schools*. Newton, MA: Allyn and Bacon, c1978.

Gibbons, Don C. *Delinquent Behavior*. Englewood Cliffs, NJ: Prentice-Hall, c1970.

Gilchrist, Robert S., and Bernice R. Roberts, et al. *Curriculum Development*. Belmont, CA: L. Siegler/Fearon, c1974.

Glasser, William. *Schools Without Failure*. New York: Harper, c1969.

Gold, Milton J., et al. *In Praise of Diversity*. Teacher Corps.

Goldstein, William, and Joseph C. DeVita. *Successful School Communications*. Englewood Cliffs, NJ: Parker, c1977.

Goodlad, John I. *A Place Called School*. New York: McGraw-Hill, c1984.

Grambs, Jean Dresden. *Intergroup Education*. Englewood Cliffs, NJ: Prentice-Hall, c1968.

Grant, Carl A. *Community Participation in Education*. Newton, MA: Allyn and Bacon, c1979.

Gross, Ronald, ed. *The Teacher and the Taught*. New York: Dell, c1963.

Hacker, Andrew, ed. *U/S: A Statistical Portrait of the American People*. New York: Viking, c1983.

Hackney, Harold, and L. Sherilyn Cormier. *Counseling Strategies and Objectives*. Englewood Cliffs, NJ: Prentice-Hall, c1979.

Hammill, Donald D., and Nettie R. Bartel. *Teaching Children with Learning and Behavior Problems*. Newton, MA: Allyn and Bacon, c1975.

Handbook for Youth-Centered Leadership. Future Homemakers of America, c1982.

Handicapped Funding Directory: 1988–89. 6th ed. Research Grant Guides, c1988.

Harrison, Charles H. *Schoolgirl Pregnancy.* National School Public Relations Association, c1972.

Hassett, Joseph D., and Arline Weisberg. *Open Education.* Englewood Cliffs, NJ: Prentice-Hall, c1972.

Herbert, Cindy. *Everychild's Everyday.* New York: Doubleday, c1980.

Hertzberg, Alvin, and Edward F. Stone. *Schools Are for Children.* New York: Schocken, c1971.

Herzberg, Frederick. *Work and the Nature of Man.* Cleveland, OH: World, c1966.

Hewett, Frank M., and Steven R. Forness. *Education of Exceptional Learners.* Newton, MA: Allyn & Bacon, c1974.

Hilgard, Ernest Ropiequet, and Gordon H. Bower. *Theories of Learning.* 3d ed. New York: Appleton-Century-Crofts, c1966.

Hirsch, E. D. *Cultural Literacy.* Boston, MA: Houghton, 1987.

Holt, John Caldwell. *The Underachieving School.* New York: Pitman, c1969.

Howard, Eugene R. *School Discipline Desk Book.* Englewood Cliffs, NJ: Parker, c1978.

Howe, Harold. *Picking Up the Options.* National Education Association, c1968.

Hudgins, H. C., and Richard S. Vacca. *Law and Education: Contemporary Issues and Court Decisions.* Charlottesville, VA: Michie, c1979.

Huggett, Albert John, and T. M. Stinnett. *Professional Problems of Teachers.* 2d ed. New York: Macmillan, c1963.

Hunter, Madeline. *Improved Instruction.* TIP Publications, c1976.

————. *Mastery Teaching.* TIP Publications, c1982.

Hyde, Margaret Oldroyd. *My Friend Has Four Parents.* New York: McGraw-Hill, c1981.

Ideas for Improving Public Confidence in Public Education... National School Public Relations Association.

Jensema, Carl J., and Raymond J. Trybus. *Communication Patterns and Educational Achievement of Hearing Impaired Students.* ODS.

Jersild, Arthur Thomas. *Child Psychology.* 6th ed. Englewood Cliffs, NJ: Prentice-Hall, c1968.

Jeter, Katherine F. *These Special Children.* Palo Alto, CA: Bull, c1982.

Jewett, Claudia L. *Helping Children Cope with Separation and Loss.* Boston, MA: Harvard Common Pr., c1982.

Keef, James W. *Instructional Leadership Handbook.* National Association of Secondary School Principals, c1984.

Kelley, Edgar A. *Improving School Climate.* Natinal Association of Secondary School Principals, c1980.

Kempe, Charles Henry, and Ray E. Helfer, eds. *Helping the Battered Child and His Family.* Philadelphia: Lippincott, c1972.

Keniston, Kenneth. *All Our Children.* New York: Harcourt, c1977.

Keys to Innovative Educational Practices. National Association of State Advisory Councils, c1977.

Kindred, Leslie Withrow, Don Bagin, and Donald R. Gallagher. *The School and Community Relations.* Englewood Cliffs, NJ: Prentice-Hall, c1976.

Lagrand, Louis E. *Discipline in the Secondary School.* West Nyack, NY: Parker, c1969.

Lemke, Elmer. *Principles of Psychological Measurement.* Boston, MA: Houghton Mifflin, c1976.

Leonard, George Burr. *Education and Ecstasy.* New York: Delacorte, c1968.

Lightfoot, Sara Lawrence. *The Good High School.* New York: Basic Books, c1983.

Lovejoy's College Guide. New York: Simon and Schuster, c1970.

Lovejoy's Prep School Guide, 1958–. New York: Harper, 1968.

McCarthy, Martha M., and Nelda H. Cambron. *Public School Law.* Newton, MA: Allyn & Bacon, c1981.

McKibbin, Michael, et al. *Teaching and Learning.* Association of Teacher Educators, c1977.

McNeil, John D. *Curriculum: A Comprehensive Introduction.* Boston, MA: Little, Brown and Company, c1985.

Massey, Morris E. *The People Puzzle.* Boston, MA: Boston, c1979.

Medeiros, Donald C., Barbara J. Porter, and I. David Welch. *Children Under Stress.* Englewood Cliffs, NJ: Prentice-Hall, c1983.

Morrow, Gertrude. *The Compassionate School.* Englewood Cliffs, NJ: Prentice-Hall, c1987.

National School Public Relations Association. *Putting Words and Pictures About Schools Into Print.* Washington, DC, c1971.

Neill, Alexander Sutherland. *Summerhill.* New York: Hart, c1960.

Offer, Daniel. *The Psychological World of the Teen-Ager.* New York: Basic Books, c1969.

O'Leary, K. Daniel, and Susan G. O'Leary. *Classroom Management.* Elmsford, NY: Pergamon, c1972.

Parks, A. Lee, and Marilyn K. Rousseau. *The Public Law Supporting Mainstreaming.* Learning Concepts, c1977.

Patterson, Gerald R. *Living with Children.* Champaign, IL: Research Press, c1976.

Peter, Laurence J. *Prescriptive Teaching.* New York: McGraw, c1965.

Podolsky, Arthur, et al. *Education Directory.* Washington, DC: U.S. Government Printing Office, c1976.

Ravitch, Diane. *The Troubled Crusade.* New York: Basic Books, c1983.

Rawson, Margaret B. *A Bibliography on the Nature, Recognition and Treatment of Language Difficulties.* Orton Society, c1972.

Redl, Fritz, and David Winemann. *The Aggressive Child.* Glencoe, IL: Free Press, c1957.

Reutter, E. Edmund. *Schools and the Law.* Dobbs Ferry, NY: Oceana, c1981.

Rhodes, Eric F., and Robert A. Smith. *Collective Bargaining Problems in Colleges and Universities.* Educational Service Bureau, c1977.

Rohrlick, Paula. *Exploring the Arts.* Bowker, c1982.

Schinke, Steven Paul. *Life Skills Counseling with Adolescents.* University Park Press, c1984.

Seltz, Reynolds C. *Law and the School Principal.* Cincinnati, OH: W. H. Anderson, c1961.

Sequel, Mary Louise. *The Curriculum Field.* New York: Teachers College Press, c1966.

Siberman, Charles E. *Crisis in the Classroom.* 1st ed. New York: Random House, c1970.

Simon, Kenneth A., et al. *Projections of Education Statistics to 1984–85.* Washington, DC: U.S. Department of Health, Education, and Welfare.

Skinner, Burrhus Frederic. *The Technology of Teaching.* New York: Appleton-Century-Crofts, c1968.

Smith, Robert M. *Clinical Teaching.* 2d ed. New York: McGraw, c1974.

Stelzer, Leigh. *Teachers Have Rights, Too.* ERIC Clearinghouse for Social Studies, c1980.

Stephens, Thomas M., and Joan S. Wolf. *Effective Skills in Parent/Teacher Conferencing.* NCEMMH/OSU, c1980.

Stevenson, Harold W. *Child Psychology.* University of Chicago Press, c1963.

Straughn, Charles T., and Barbarasue Lovejoy Straughn, eds. *Lovejoy's College Guide.* 16th ed. Monarch, c1983.

Strope, John L., Jr. *School Activities and the Law.* The National Association of Secondary School Principals, c1984.

Sulzer-Azaroff, Beth. *Applying Behavioral Analysis.* CBS College Publishing, c1982.

Swanson, B. Marian, and Diane J. Willis. *Understanding Exceptional Children and Youth.* Skokie, IL: Rand McNally, c1979.

Sylvester, Robert. *Common Sense in Classroom Relations.* West Nyack, NY: Parker, c1966.

Taxonomy of Educational Objectives. New York: McKay, c1964, c1984.

Thiagarajan, Sivasailam. *The Programming Process; A Practical Guide.* Charles A. Jones, c1971.

Three Views of Competency-Based Teacher Education. Bloomington, IN: Phi Delta Kappa Educational Foundation, c1974.

Trump, J. Lloyd. *A School for Everyone.* National Association of Secondary School Principals, c1977.

Unruh, Adolph, and Harold E. Turner. *Supervision for Change and Innovation.* Boston, MA: Houghton, c1970.

Wallace, Gerald, and Stephen C. Larsen. *Educational Assessment of Learning Problems.* Newton, MA: Allyn & Bacon, c1978.

Ward, Colin, comp. *Vandalism.* New York: Van Nostrand Reinhold, c1973.

Whaley, Nita B. *School Volunteers.* National School Public Relations Association, c1973.

Wiederholt, J. Lee, ed. *Historical Perspectives on the Education of the Learning Disabled.* Tucson: University of Arizona.

Wilson, L. Craig. *The Open Access Curriculum.* Newton, MA: Allyn & Bacon, c1971.

_____. *School Leadership Today.* Newton, MA: Allyn & Bacon, c1978.

Wolfgang, Charles H. *Solving Discipline Problems.* Newton, MA: Allyn & Bacon, c1980.

Woodring, Paul. *Investment in Innovation.* 1st ed. Boston, MA: Little, Brown, c1970.

Wyne, Marvin D., and Peter D. O'Connor. *Exceptional Children.* Lexington, MA: Heath, c1979.

Wynne, Edward A. *Looking at Schools.* Lexington, MA: Lexington Books, c1980.

Index